The Intentional Leader

The Intentional Leader

Kenneth A. Shaw

With a Foreword by James L. Fisher

 Syracuse University Press

Copyright © 2005 by Syracuse University Press
Syracuse, New York 13244–5160
All Rights Reserved

First Edition 2005
06 07 08 09 10   6 5 4 3 2

The paper used in this publication meets the minimum requirements of
American National Standard for Information Sciences—Permanence of
Paper for Printed Library Materials, ANSI Z39.48–1984.∞™

Library of Congress Cataloging-in-Publication Data
Shaw, Kenneth A.
The intentional leader / Kenneth A. Shaw ; with a foreword by James L. Fisher.— 1st ed.
p. cm.
Includes bibliographical references and index.
ISBN 0–8156–3086–7 (alk. paper)
1. Leadership. I. Title.
HD57.7.S48 2005
658.4'092—dc22   2005016315

Manufactured in the United States of America

We are dependent on leaders at many levels and in all segments of our society—business, government, organized labor, agriculture, the professions, the minority communities, the arts, the universities, social services, and so on. . . . If it weren't for this wide dispersal of leadership, our kind of society couldn't function.

—John Gardner, *On Leadership*

Kenneth "Buzz" Shaw served as a campus or system president for twenty-seven years at Southern Illinois University, the University of Wisconsin system, and Syracuse University, where he spent his last thirteen years as a university leader. Shaw has consulted with numerous education, government, and private sector profit and nonprofit organizations and presently serves on a number of such boards.

A recipient of eight honorary degrees, Dr. Shaw was recognized by authors Fisher and Koch as one of the nation's top entrepreneurial presidents in their most recent book on the subject. Shaw authored *The Successful President* as well as more than thirty-five articles and book chapters on leadership and issues in higher education. He presently serves as Chancellor Emeritus and University Professor at Syracuse University, where he teaches leadership to graduate and undergraduate students and just about anyone else who is interested. He and his wife, Mary Ann, have three children and seven grandchildren and reside in Skaneateles, New York.

Contents

Reality, Self-Awareness, and Other Exercises

Below is a listing of reality and self-awareness exercises presented by topic. My hope is that you will use some or all of them in your leadership quest.

Reality Exercises

Foreword

James L. Fisher

"Buzz" Shaw has written the complete book on leadership. And writing a book that smoothly and effectively combines personal experience and the best thinking from those who study and practice leadership is not easy. Indeed, by my reading, it has never been done before, and Shaw has done it!

I presume to have read most of the stuff out there, and the works are either too autobiographical, though often interesting and momentarily inspiring, or far too heavy on the theoretical side, and dulling. Invariably, we are left wanting. Shaw has given us enough theory to satisfy the scholar and has translated that theory into reality through example and his extraordinary personal experience, and finally, practice exercises to test changing attitudes and learning—a complete course. All of this allows us to "be able to do leadership at a higher plane." Shaw obviously believes, as I do, that leadership can be learned, as he deftly pushes us to new heights of understanding, appreciation, and performance.

The Intentional Leader is just what it implies. If you want to lead, study, practice and perform: Do leadership! He takes us from the concise definition of leadership as a moving process of persuasion and example to discussions of emotions, conflict, power, communication, crises, different cultures, and change and ends with a powerful chapter on ethics. While in large measure

James L. Fisher is author, coauthor, or editor of ten books on leadership, notably in higher education.

he treats leadership as a generic, he thoughtfully discusses race, different cultures, and gender. Readers will be especially taken and informed by the sensitive and instructive section written by Mary Ann Shaw on women.

Finally, I shamelessly admit that this book moved me from admiration to fun to tears and back to admiration. Yes, it is the complete book on leadership, and it will endure.

Preface

Someone once said that we're all divided into one of three groups: those who want to help make things happen, those who watch things happen, and those who say, "What happened?" If you want to help make things happen, this book is for you.

You are among the millions of people our nation and the world needs — leaders. Every day, each of us has an opportunity to lead or to follow, and, as you will learn, to do both. Sometimes you'll learn from this book to be watchers, but seldom will you be a "what-happened?" person.

Whoever or wherever you are, you may be called upon to step up as a leader:

• Ada, selected by corporate management to serve on a team assigned to create a new marketing approach;

• Bill, a local United Way chairman who is facing a serious personnel problem;

• Marvin, president of a major international firm facing intense worldwide competition;

• Sally, a sergeant in the U.S. Army stationed in Afghanistan;

• Jim, member of a local fair housing board faced with serious discrimination problems in his community;

• Susan, county state's attorney;

• George, governor of a large state with serious financial problems;

• Sarah, house manager for two spirited children and a frequently out-of-town husband;

• Andrew, president of his university's student government association.

These people and millions of others have leadership opportunities daily.

Fortunately, people do step up and do so adequately—or sometimes quite well—as leaders. Others try to lead but fail badly.

I believe that each of us can become a better leader. While we are somewhat limited by heredity in everything we do, we still can learn much about leadership and apply what we learn. And we can get better.

This will be a practical approach to leadership, where I provide you with the understanding, basic skills, and practice needed to lead. You will learn what leaders do and how they do it. You will learn a great deal about yourself, as self-awareness is an important part of leadership effectiveness. You will better understand the interpersonal skills you need to lead. You will develop conflict resolution, motivational, communication, and decision-making skills. You will know the moral and effective use of power. All of this can be yours if you choose to lead.

Notice I'm using interchangeably the acquisition of information and the development of skills. I believe that understanding the nature of leadership and its required skills is not all that difficult. You will find this an easy book to understand and follow. Far more difficult will be learning how to use these understandings and skills—actually *doing* leadership. In the last analysis, it is the doing that is most important—and most difficult. I want to jumpstart the process by describing the needed tools and offering ways that you can practice them.

After looking at *you* and describing some of the interpersonal skills you will need, we will look at the importance of groups of all sizes with a multitude of goals. We will focus on running effective meetings, moving groups to make quality decisions, using various approaches to deal with medium and large size groups, learning positive group roles, and fostering creativity. Groups can be boring; they can be an enormous waste of time. They also can be extremely powerful and innovative if you master the group skills you'll be learning.

From these group encounters, we will learn about how organizations and institutions work, and how they can be transformed, given the right conditions and the right leadership. We will look at techniques for organizational renewal, offer clues for coping with organizational grief, and suggest ways to keep organizations and institutions learning and leadership focused. Effective decision making and handling crises also will be covered in that part of the book.

Then we will offer a touch of humility, both for the reader and for your author. Not everything you've learned so far will work in every situation. Leaders need to be extremely resilient. We will examine leadership in intercultural settings, describing the unique challenges and opportunities that exist in our diverse population where women and people of color are moving into leadership positions. We will also look at leadership around the world. While there are similarities in approach, there are also differences.

Finally, we will return to you, reminding you of the importance of being well-grounded so that you can lead—focusing on character and ethics, finding purpose in your life, and suggesting ways to maintain balance. In the last section, I remind you of your responsibility to teach others how to lead and offer ways you can encourage leadership development.

You will note the frequent use of quotations interspersed throughout the chapters and sections. They have been selected to illustrate points made, and in some cases, to offer opposing viewpoints. Some will come from leadership scholars, some from highly visible leaders, some from persons in middle management positions, and some from those providing day-to-day, but little-noticed leadership. Some lesser known leaders will be given pseudonyms to protect both the innocent and the guilty. Occasionally, I will turn to colleagues to offer more extensive views. By providing diverse opinions, I hope to enrich your understanding and to remind you that leadership comes in all shapes and sizes.

I've already mentioned what we are about: doing leadership. Leadership scholar Warren Bennis has noted that a lot of people want to lead but far fewer actually want to do leadership. I would add this to his important insight: among those who want to do leadership, far fewer do it well. So, as you read this book, know that understanding is important, but it will only get you to first base. Doing leadership and doing it well requires knowing and applying the skills you learn.

Is this book and our time together worth your effort? The answer is yes, if you want to be a better leader or if the mantle of leadership is forced on you and you must step up. But it is only worth it if you really want to do leadership. If that's the case, we're going to have a lot of fun together. Let's start now.

All the best.

Acknowledgments

There are many people to credit for inspiring and shaping this book—those who gave me the opportunity and encouragement to study, to "do" leadership, and to present my views to others.

I start by thanking my mentors, Bob Bone, Sam Braden, Jim Fisher, and Dick Hulet for pushing me far beyond what I thought my capabilities were. The same can be said for my professors at Illinois State University, the University of Illinois, and Purdue University.

I am also grateful to my colleagues at Towson University, Southern Illinois University, the University of Wisconsin, and Syracuse University, who put up with me while I received on-the-job leadership training.

My thanks also go to the many insightful people who have studied and written about leadership. Their insights have guided my writing, and more important, my conduct as a leader.

Also, I have been blessed to know as colleagues and friends leaders in education, business, government, and the not-for-profit sector. Many were good enough to provide their views on intentional leadership for this book. I have learned a great deal from them, and I hope I sent a few good ideas their way.

Syracuse has so many talented people who provided assistance. Faculty colleagues Dennis Gillen, David Rubin, Joe Shedd, Bill Coplin and Gerry Grant shared with me their favorite leadership books, allowing me to provide the leader with references representing a variety of fields and points of view.

I also had help from some of the finest students in the country. Kate Eby did an excellent job of reference checking and preparing the list of readings. Brendan Kneram provided all the illustrations for the book. Three students, Chris Demo, Jen Feldon and Alys Mann, read an early manuscript, offered suggestions for improving the exercises, and posed some of the questions that I have attempted to answer in the appendix. I predict great futures for these fine young people.

Others have made remarkable contributions by their encouragement and involvement. Dennis Byrne read, edited, and challenged me to get it right. He, Jeff Unaitis, Barry Wells, and Mary Ann Shaw added their written insights on topics requiring other perspectives.

And to Gretchen Goldstein, special thanks for typing the first two drafts of the manuscript late at night and on weekends. Thanks to you, Kathy Pitt, for putting the finishing touches on the challenging questions/short answers section in the appendix. Peter Webber and the staff of the Syracuse University Press were most helpful to me every step of the way. I am very grateful for your professionalism and sensitivity.

I also want to thank Syracuse University for providing me with a leave of absence and the Nason Foundation for underwriting much of the cost. You made this book possible.

Finally, thanks to Mary Ann Shaw, my wife, best friend, and valued colleague, whose love, encouragement and support gave me the motivation to complete this project. And to Ken, Susan, and Sara and their spouses and children—no better people, no better friends. I am truly blessed.

The Intentional Leader

1

Here Are My Biases

Leadership isn't about position; it's about behavior.
—James M. Kouzes and Barry Z. Posner,
The Leadership Challenge

In fairness to you, I'll begin by putting my biases on the table. You may want to refer to them as you read other parts of the book.

You can learn to lead. It helps to have natural gifts, but learned understandings and skills can make us better leaders. Even those with a special talent for leadership can get better. My goal is to get you from where you are now to a higher leadership plane.

So, leaders are both born and made—I submit mostly made. Think of the self-aware person who realizes his weaknesses in speaking before large groups. He can learn various techniques of speaking, practice them before friendly observers, and receive constructive suggestions. He can strive to get better. We will follow this pattern often in our journey—that is, learning understandings, learning the skills, and then applying them. And the more you apply them, the better you get.

Leaders are followers, too. Often situations require us to play any number of roles in life—sometimes as designated leaders, sometimes as informal leaders, and sometimes as supportive followers. In my life I've had many opportunities to seize the mantle of formal leadership. But I'm also a member of groups where it is better that I be a loyal and supportive follower. One community group in particular has an amazingly talented leader whom I strongly support and follow. In this instance I occasionally find myself participating as

1

an informal leader, but clearly my role in this situation is to follow. And I do, gladly.

Positional leaders are extremely important. These are the people with the big titles, such as governor or president of a university. When positional leaders lead well, we are indeed fortunate. When they don't, our fragile institutions begin to erode. While positional leaders are extremely important, we tend to give them less flexibility than was once the case.

Informal leaders are also extremely important. Often, they are the true leaders of a group or institution. Think about instances when someone's historical knowledge, technical expertise, or simple ability to get things done come forward in a group. As you will learn, leadership takes many forms, and informal leaders are in many ways as important as positional leaders.

Leaders, both positional and informal, need to be well grounded. The flaws of our positional leaders in particular become obvious quite soon. Thus, a sense of self-awareness, personal values, and the way we balance our complex lives becomes very important. This is why we will spend so much time on *you*—helping you to learn more about yourself, your strengths and weaknesses, and how you might make maximum use of your unique qualities.

I want you to be a just, moral leader. Make no mistake; some solid leaders are amoral, or worse. Leadership experts such as James McGregor Burns[1] believe a good leader is someone who has laudable goals and the ability to move people in a moral direction. That's what I want from you. However, to be fair, others such as Barbara Kellerman,[2] aver that leadership is not necessarily a moral concept—that we can learn even from the most malevolent leaders. We won't be entering into the debate over whether Hitler and Stalin were good leaders. For our purposes, we will talk only about effective leaders. The guarantee that these leadership skills will be used for only good, moral purposes will have to come from you.

Leadership is often fun, but not always. It can be stimulating, extremely satisfying, and often ego gratifying. It can also be extremely frustrating, sometimes boring, and often stressful. Leaders must enjoy seeing good things happen. You will soon learn, however, that it isn't always fun.

1. James MacGregor Burns, *Leadership* (San Francisco: Jossey-Bass, 1996).
2. Barbara Kellerman, "Leadership: Warts and All," *Harvard Business Review,* Jan. 2004.

There is no one standard way of leading. I will be teaching you under-standings and skills that I believe work most of the time. But they don't work for all situations, so I've provided introductory and sidebar comments from successful leaders and scholars in the field, and also included sections on dealing with intercultural and other experiences. In the last analysis, we all do what works for us. Quite honestly, this book is about what has worked for me. You will see quotes that illustrate points I wish to make, but this work is about my philosophy of leadership, grounded mainly in reading and in my experi-ences—not from empirical study.

To be a good leader, you need also to be at least an adequate manager (and sometimes better than that). As I said before, you also must be able to follow sometimes. I repeat this point to be sure you understand it and also to illustrate the complexities of leadership.

Myths about leadership are abundant, but not important. We won't spend a lot of time on the numerous myths about leadership. But you should know they exist. For example, Komives[3] cites an ancient Greek myth that asserts that a man, to lead, must have a potbelly. Others insist that leadership is just good common sense. Still others debate whether men or women are more effective. None of these myths will get in our way. My premise is that *you* can become a better leader and the rest is less important.

Finally, *leadership is doing.* Warren Bennis[4] described an epiphany that came to him after more than a decade as a higher education leader. "The truth is I didn't have the passion for it. . . . I wanted to be a university presi-dent. I didn't want to *do* university president." This book is about doing lead-ership. I will be pleased if some of you learn what's in the book and choose not to apply it. But my real purpose is to aid those of you who want to learn and do. Daniel Goleman[5] correctly believes that the key to learning new habits is practicing to the point of mastery, which means effective repetition making the practices as lifelike as possible. I once allowed my ego to get the best of me.

3. Susan R. Komives, Nancy Lucas, and Timothy R. McMahon, *Exploring Leadership: For College Students Who Want to Make a Difference* (San Francisco: Jossey-Bass, 1998), 27.

4. Warren Bennis, "An Invented Life: Shoe Polish, Milli Vanilli and Sapiential Circles," in *An Invented Life* (Reading, Mass.: Addison-Wesley, 1993), 81.

5. Daniel Goleman, Richard Boyatzis, and Annie McKee, *Primal Leadership: Learning to Lead with Emotional Intelligence* (Boston: Harvard Business School Press, 2004).

I accepted a challenge to run a one-mile race—no easy task, then, for a middle-age person, slightly overweight and never good at distance running. But I practiced. I ran a lot of miles trying to reduce my time. I also ran quarter-miles for speed and longer distances for endurance. My time wasn't great (5:52), but it was about two minutes faster than when I had started six weeks earlier. It's that level of doing—practice, repetition—that allows us to move from understanding to actually possessing the skill to do leadership.

Enough on my biases. In the next section you will learn what leaders do and begin the task ahead. Let's get going.

2

Leadership Defined and Explained

*But of a good leader, who talks little, when his work is
done, his aims fulfilled, they will all say: "we did this
ourselves."*

—Lao-Tzu

In this chapter we define leadership and discuss the tasks of leaders, including
leadership frames — the different ways to view leadership.

Leadership Defined

First, a workable definition of leadership. Here I turn to John Gardner[1]
and Ronald Haifetz,[2] and my modest additions to their thinking. *Leadership
is a process of persuasion and example, by which others are motivated to take
action.* That's easy enough to understand. Note the emphasis on persuasion,
example, and taking action, as I will frequently refer to these activities. As
with most definitions, a few "yes, buts" are needed for clarification. Although
leaders do persuade others, as we mentioned in the introduction, others also
persuade them. Leaders, then, must understand the mission, values, and
vision of the institutions and groups with whom they work. Leaders give
and take.

As Haifetz states, influencing others to act means that the tough problems

1. John W. Gardner, *On Leadership* (New York: Free Press, 1990).
2. Ronald Haifetz, *Leadership Without Easy Answers* (Cambridge, Mass.: Harvard Univ.
Press, 2003).

are tackled. The effective leader helps to clarify what matters most and helps others to understand and to deal with trade-offs.

Effective leaders, then, do more than motivate others to take action on the easy things. Haifetz calls the work of leaders "adaptive work." That means that our effectiveness as leaders is measured by our efforts and the results of those efforts—getting people to address *real* problems in a *real* way.

Reality Exercise. Think of a person you know who best exemplifies this definition, someone who persuades, and by example, induces others to move toward action—taking on the difficult challenges— while being sensitive to institutional and personal needs. Think about formal leaders you know who don't fit this definition. Name some of them. Is the definition too limiting or are some "formal" leaders simply not true leaders?

What Leaders Do

> *The foundation of effective leadership is thinking*
> *through the organization's mission, defining it, and*
> *establishing it clearly and visibly.*
> — Peter Drucker, *The Essential Drucker*

Leaders *do* leadership in four major ways. They:
  Envision and affirm mission, goals, and values,
  Articulate mission, goals, and values,
  Implement mission, goals, and values, and
  Serve as the keeper of mission, goals, and values.

Envisioning and Affirming Mission, Goals, and Values

Someone has to point us in the right direction. Otherwise we are like the pilot lost over Newfoundland who radios back that he's lost, but he's making record time. Lou Gerstner, IBM chair, reminds us that any road taken gets us to the same place if we don't know where we are going.[3] This visioning process generally does not occur through an overnight epiphany. Often, mission, goals, and values exist, but not in writing. The leader may have a strong hand in establishing them, but they generally come from the combined thoughts of many.

For example, in higher education everyone — motivated by different needs — seems to be doing something different. Students busily study, form friendships, and have fun — although not necessarily in that order. Faculty members occupy themselves with their courses, scholarship, and, of course, parking. But a university president is charged with defining the overall vision and guarding the institution's core values. His rooftop view is one that others, too busy trying to meet their own responsibilities, miss. Some examples from *Business: The Ultimate Resource*[4] will help explain the importance of this task.

---

3. Louis V. Gerstner, Jr., *Who Says Elephants Can't Dance?: Inside IBM's Historic Turnaround* (New York: HarperBusiness, 2002).

4. *Business: The Ultimate Resource.* New York: Perseus Publishing, 2002.

We note how successful business leaders have used their vision to guide their companies.

Michael Dell, chairman and CEO of Dell Computers, built his company's business model around a unique vision requiring little capital: build products to order, using the Internet as an inexpensive, efficient, direct link to customers. Pretty simple — and it worked.

Berkshire Hathaway CEO Warren Buffett's vision is to invest in undervalued companies with low overhead costs, high growth potential, strong market share, and low price-to-earnings ratios. Buffett's vision has certainly worked for him!

Herb Kelleher's vision for Southwest Airlines when he established it in 1971 included two key principles: keep customers happy and keep costs down.

In 1955, the late Ray Kroc built his McDonald's fast-food empire on four pillars: quality, service, cleanliness, and value.

When I came to Syracuse University, I talked and listened to hundreds of people. Those conversations made clear to me what our institutional values were, even though they were not in writing. They were quality, innovation, caring, diversity, and service. When I spoke of them at my inaugural convocation, the reaction was, "ah-hah!" Everyone knew these values were right for us, even though they had been unstated until then.

Later, as we negotiated a very serious financial restructuring period, I announced that our mission was to be *the* outstanding student-centered research university. That also resonated well and prompted a variety of initiatives that I'll explain later.

Yes, the vision thing is important.

> "Vision and direction are essential for greatness. In world-class organizations everyone has a clear sense where the organization is going. Only when the leaders in an organization know their people understand the agreed-upon vision and direction can they attend to the organization's ability to deliver on that vision."
> —Ken Blanchard and Jesse Stoner, *Leader to Leader*, 2004

Articulating Mission, Goals, and Values

Even the best ideas die on the vine if they're not communicated effectively and often. The leader's job is to make certain that these messages are carried by every means available. Kotter[5] believes that undercommunicating the vision stifles innovation. He describes an organization that developed a good vision but communicated it by holding just a single meeting and sending out a series of written messages, using a miniscule 0.001 percent of the company's yearly internal communications. It didn't take. A second, more vigorous approach was equally ineffective. The head of the organization spent considerable time speaking to employee groups in addition to the written communications, but most people still didn't get it—not surprising, since the vision captured about only 0.005 percent of total yearly communications.

Such efforts are important enough, but much more needs to be done. What we *do* communicates tons about what is important. The mission is more apt to take if, in addition to repeating it, we actually reinforce it with our decisions.

Effective communicators also make good use of storytelling—using examples from the organization that illustrate the vision. One very successful college president, James L. Fisher, who led Towson State University for ten years, used the coffeepot approach to storytelling. At least once a week he hit some of the major coffeepots on the growing campus. For several hours, he saw and talked with staff, faculty, and students who happened to be around the coffeepot. The discussions often involved individual personal issues but invariably led to larger university issues. He viewed these discussions as important opportunities to communicate his approachability and to receive direct, unfiltered information about what's going on at the university. In addition, it gave him an opportunity to tell "the story," using examples of how his vision for the university played out in real life. Fisher was open and friendly, but he remained presidential during the encounters.

At Syracuse University, I often used brief paper communications called Buzzwords, which we later put on the Web. I covered a variety of important is-

5. John P. Kotter, *Leading Change* (Cambridge, Mass.: Harvard Business School Press, 1996), 3.

sues, such as diversity, athletics, civility, quality management, managing change, and working in teams. People were invited to comment, and I attempted to answer each response. This was a way for me to tell my story and to learn from other sources.

In other settings, I often brought together a random group of staff, faculty, and students for a brown-bag discussion. Together, we settled on a half-dozen topics for our chat. Taking one at a time, I heard their views, tried to summarize when a consensus existed, and then gave my view, which led to further discussion. I learned a great deal from people I would not have encountered otherwise, and they had a chance to hear me "tell the story."

Another university president regularly opened her office on Friday afternoons for half-hour meetings to discuss issues, ideas, or concerns with members of the university community. In the first few years, she was heavily booked, with many people bringing their problems to her. It turned out that many problems were not caused by the organization, but some were, and change occurred. These meetings communicated very quickly that she meant business.

One corporate leader uses the employee cafeteria to learn about what was going on and to tell his story. It was his way of managing by walking around. Sometimes he planned the cafeteria meetings; often he would venture in alone. He feels that it helped him to break down barriers between managers and their subordinates as other top people began to eat in the cafeteria. It became a great place to test new ideas, to assess the general mood, and of course to tell the story.

Often, we get so excited about telling our story that we forget our audiences. We make the story too long and complex. Kotter[6] offers excellent advice: "If you can't communicate the vision to someone in five minutes or less and get a reaction that signifies both an understanding and interest, you won't be able to move your organization or group toward transforming change."

Finally, Fred Greenstein[7] has carefully researched the leadership effectiveness of American presidents. He concludes that Woodrow Wilson was the

6. Kotter, *Leading Change*.

7. Fred Greenstein, "The Leadership Qualities of Effective Presidents: FDR to George W. Bush," Center for Public Leadership, Conversations on Leadership, 2000–2001.

"Language is among the most powerful methods for expressing a vision. Successful leaders use metaphors and figures of speech; they give examples, tell stories, and relate anecdotes; they draw word pictures that offer quotations and they recite slogans."
— James M. Kouzes and Barry Z. Posner, *Leadership Challenges*

first to use rhetorical skill to tell a story. Wilson introduced a new tradition of appearing before Congress in person and delivering the State of the Union Address. In it, he proposed a "new freedom" program for the country.

Franklin Delano Roosevelt surpassed Wilson by setting *the* standard for public communication. His inspiration of the American public during the Great Depression and World War II led actor/director Orson Welles to call him "the second-best actor in America"—after Welles himself. Greenstein also identified John F. Kennedy as an effective presidential communicator, particularly in giving formal speeches. Which of us who grew up hearing his memorable words, "Ask what you can do for your country," can ever forget them?

And there's Ronald Reagan, the great communicator, who earned his reputation as the "Teflon president" for his ability to escape sticky situations unscathed. Reagan forcefully and simply communicated his vision: cut the size of the federal government, cut taxes, and rid the world of communism. He stuck on that agenda and communicated his views repeatedly.

Communications, then, take on a variety of forms. The effective leader tries to use them all.

Implementing Mission, Goals, and Values

Implementing the mission is often called management. If we don't implement, nothing's going to happen. Gerstner reminds us that we shouldn't be credited for predicting rain. Building an ark is another matter. In other words, good ideas from articulate people aren't enough.

In my earlier days as a president, long before it was easy to obtain information from the Web, I excitedly waited for a nationally noted college president to deliver his annual speech to the faculty. His ideas were visionary, and he spoke with compassion and eloquence. I waited for a published copy to see which of his great ideas I might implement. Ironically and sadly, this president's institution implemented few of these great ideas because of a lack of follow-through. On the other hand, Michael Dell maintains close contact with his company, even occasionally manning the customer hotline to hear firsthand what people say about his products.[8] And he utilizes a 360-degree evaluation process in which employees, including him, are reviewed by those above and below.

Buffett prides himself on hiring strong direct reports, seeing them as excellent long-term investments. He rarely contacts his operating executives, but he knows what's going on, and they know they can call him whenever he's needed. Herb Kelleher often travels on Southwest Airlines simply to hear what customers are saying. During Kroc's lifetime, his McDonald's restaurants, even though franchises, followed strict and uniform guidelines. A central laboratory ensured consistency in the food's preparation, down to the exact water content in those French fries.

Much of skilled managing means the ability to identify, nurture, and motivate people. Charan and Colvin[9] say top leaders most often blow it when they fail to put the right people in the right jobs or when they fail to fix people problems in time. Specifically, they find leaders who are unwilling or unable to deal with those who aren't with the program. Everyone knows there's a problem, but nothing gets done.

Colin Powell, in discussing the lessons he learned in leadership, reminds us that we can never neglect details. "When everyone's mind is dulled or distracted, the leader must be doubly vigilant. All the great ideas and visions in the world are worthless if they can't be implemented rapidly and efficiently. Good leaders delegate and empower others, but they pay attention to details, every day."[10] And, of course, Powell believes, as many of us do, that all the plans in the world would come to naught if it were not for people who make things happen.

8. *Business: The Ultimate Resource.*

9. Ram Charan and Geoffrey Colvin, "Why CEOs Fail," *Fortune,* June 21, 1999, 69.

10. Harari, Oren, *The Leadership Secrets of Colin Powell* (New York: McGraw-Hill, 2002), 257.

Finally, in managing people, Bennis and Collingwood[11] argue, leaders make a big mistake by becoming overly involved with the sickest members of a group. "Forced to the sidelines of the confrontation and envious of the attention lavished on the sickest members, the healthier members will begin to resent you and question the legitimacy of your leadership." They describe the experiences of Deborah Kasatos, senior vice president for human resources at Charles Schwab and Company. She observed that when a company launches a change initiative, employees divide into three groups: evangelists, who eagerly support the change initiative; passive observers, who neither support nor oppose the initiative but wait to see what's going to happen; and "squeaky wheels," who for a variety of reasons vocally oppose any change. Too often, she says, the leaders focus on the "squeaky wheels" and ignore the others, particularly the passive observers. Since they are strongly influenced by their relationships with their leader, they can easily go the other way.

Have I overdone the management thing? I don't think so. Not all of us are great managers, but we can't be lousy ones. And we need to assess just how good we are at managing change and our key people.

Serving as the Keeper of the Mission, Goals, and Values

Those in leadership positions are the conscience of the group. That means asking hard questions. It means foregoing some opportunities in favor of others for the long-term good of the institution or group. It doesn't necessarily make people happy, but it is necessary.

As we went through financial restructuring at Syracuse University, we reduced our base budget by $60 million. We could have cut uniformly across the board, but that would have sent the wrong message. Cuts were made selectively, with heavier reductions falling on administration and even deeper cuts on underperforming units. Guiding us in these cuts were our values and our mission to be the leading student-centered research university.

Ray Kroc, when he was in charge of the McDonald's empire, operated by the principle that everyone would profit or no one would. It meant that he

11. Warren Bennis and Harris Collingwood, "Conquer and Divide," *Compass: A Journal of Leadership*, (Cambridge, Mass.: JFK Center at Harvard Univ.).

didn't charge his franchisees a markup on supplies and equipment, a practice that cost him a great deal at first but obviously paid off in the long run.

In today's parlance this is called walking the talk. Our best communication, which no marketing firm can do for us, comes from our ability to be genuine in what we do. The best way to ensure that the tasks of leadership are completed is to make decisions and conduct ourselves in ways that enhance our vision, mission, and values.

> *Reality Exercise.* Think of successful leaders you know. It could be someone in the public eye or someone who quietly leads without recognition but in situations where good leadership is happening. Do they apply the four tasks of leaders, and how well do they perform each? What other things, not included in the four tasks I've presented, are a part of their successful leadership?

> *Self-Awareness Exercise.* Throughout our time together, you will have opportunities to think about yourself in relation to what you're learning. Now, after learning the four tasks, think about which are your strongest and which need some work. What might you do to strengthen, overall, your potential to lead in these four tasks?

Leadership Frames

So far we've learned the four things that leaders do. But your style is also important, and it must coincide with the needs of the situation. Leaders are successful when the leadership approach and the needs of the situation are in harmony. People then say, "She is the right person for the time." Bolman and Deal[12] describe the importance of this match using several historical examples.

Winston Churchill was considered a mediocre leader early in his career when he dealt with domestic issues. Then, during World War II, he became one of the world's most inspiring and effective leaders.

Consider China. Bolman and Deal reminded me that when communists

---

12. Lee G. Bolman and Terrence E. Deal, "Reframing Leadership," in *Business Leadership*, ed. James M. Kouzes (San Francisco: Jossey-Bass, 2003).

> "Great managers may be charismatic or dull, generous or tight-fisted, visionary or numbers-oriented. But every effective executive follows eight simple practices: (1) they ask, 'What needs to be done?' (2) they ask, 'what is right for the enterprise?' (3) they develop action plans; (4) they take responsibility for decisions; (5) they take responsibility for communicating; (6) they focus on opportunities rather than problems; (7) they run productive meetings; (8) they think and say 'we,' rather than 'I.'"
>
> —Peter Drucker, *The Effective Executive*

were fighting for power in the 1930s and 1940s, they needed a visionary leader. That was Mao Tse-tung. He provided the necessary vision and inspiration for the creation of a new world order, albeit ruthlessly. Yet, by the 1970s, the importance of the Mao-style ideology had faded. A new situation—the need for economic and social development—called for more pragmatism, which often meant deviating from Mao's revolutionary vision. Enter Deng Xiaoping, who set the stage for China to create a market-based version of communism. If Mao still was in charge, such apostasy undoubtedly would have led to Deng's imprisonment, if not murder.

Lyndon Johnson provides another example of the situation meeting the times. Johnson, the consummate political insider, moved members of Congress to pass the most transforming civil rights legislation in American history. For that cause, he was the right person for the time. But on the world front, Johnson was a disaster, escalating U.S. involvement in Vietnam. It was his demise as a political leader.

So, our approach must be in sync with the situation's needs. The good leader learns the situation and knows himself or herself well enough to adapt as necessary. The good leader knows not to try to lead where his temperament or skills will fail.

What are these leadership styles? Bolman and Deal list four images (or "frames") of leadership. Each frame plays an important role and can be successful under the right conditions. They are: structural, human resources, political, and symbolic.

Structural Leaders

Structural leaders focus on designing and building an organization, a team, or some other group. Bolman and Deal refer to them as the "analysts" and the "architects." They focus on building the best structure to get things done. They lead through analysis and design. They do their homework and continually think about the relationship of structure, strategy, and the environment. They focus on implementation. They continually experiment, trying to make things better, and are open to change. Giants in the automobile industry, such as General Motors' Alfred P. Sloan, Jr., and Henry Ford, who democratized the automobile, were brilliant structural leaders.

Although the structural component is extremely important in many businesses, it may be less useful in the political arena for reasons mentioned below. Mostly, though, any organization or group will have rough going if it neglects the structural aspect. Structural leaders can be extremely effective, but they also can go overboard. The extreme structural leader will be seen as dictatorial, petty, and obsessed with detail. Attempting to rule by fiat, she has thought through everything, and knows what needs to be done. For many situations, the structural leader is perfect—our economy has thrived because of them. But not for every situation!

Human Resources Leaders

Human resources leaders view themselves as facilitators, catalysts—there to motivate and empower others. They typically advocate openness and are good listeners. Bolman and Deal believe that successful human resources leaders believe in people, try to be visible and accessible, and strive to empower others. In today's world, it's hard to imagine successful corporate, university, or nonprofit leadership without the human resources dimension. Without being sensitive to people's needs, it is hard to inspire and motivate them.

However, in its extreme, human resources leaders are seen as weaklings, creating a "feel-good" environment where little gets done. It is difficult to imagine successful organizations and groups under the management of an extreme human resources leader—unless they are service clubs or the fortunate few businesses that flourish when employees are allowed to do their own thing, in their own time. Most businesses, however, would eventually go bust. There is more to corporate success than a happy workforce.

Political Leaders

Political leaders know the importance of getting a "buy in" from individuals and groups that can help make things happen. They know how to network and work the system. They know how to give favors and how to receive them in return. Bolman and Deal describe automobile executive Lee Iacocca as a political leader. He was able to sell the idea that government intervention to save Chrysler was not only good for Chrysler but also good for America — no easy task.

Of course, people in elective positions are required to be effective political leaders, but as the Iacocca example shows, politics is everywhere — in the office, the community, and even the church. Potentially a very important skill, the political dimension also can backfire, as the leader who uses it can come off as being manipulative and dishonest.

Symbolic Leaders

Symbolic leaders inspire us to act by their words and manner, as did Dr. Martin Luther King, Jr., Franklin Roosevelt, Ronald Reagan, and Winston Churchill. They appeal to our emotions, using symbols to capture our attention. They tell their story in an inspiring way. Their vision is easy to understand and is communicated masterfully. When they finish with us, we want to march in their support. Most successful political figures are well aware of this frame and use it. The governor in a northern state taking a brief vacation in Florida knows that a blinding snowstorm requires her to return home as soon as possible — even at the risk of life. Not that she, personally, can do anything about the snow, but she needs to be there — to be seen, to encourage.

When President George W. Bush came to the destroyed Twin Towers site to thank the rescuers, he engaged in a symbolic act that strengthened his role as president. It inspired both workers and survivors. Effective symbolic leaders can move people to great things. But ineffective symbolic leaders are seen as fanatics or fools, having little substance.

Now for a little self-disclosure. How do these frames apply to my role as a university president? First, I find that different situations require different uses of the frames. For example, immediately after September 11, 2001, the symbolic frame was extremely important. While we spent considerable time dealing with the aftermath's immediate challenges, I had to be very visible and supportive. We had convocations and daily briefings in person and over the Web, and I made numerous visits to gathering places. At that time, symbolic leadership counted for about 70 percent of my efforts. In a typical year, I spent about 30 percent of my time on symbolic matters. My reason for spending this much time was my belief that, particularly in large institutions, people want to know someone is in charge and performing the expected leadership roles. People want their highly visible leaders to act like leaders.

My position also required me to be a political leader, internally and externally. Internally, it is important to balance campus constituencies to find workable solutions to problems. I also needed to work with a board of trustees, key donors, and top local, state, and national politicians. So the political frame counted for about 25 percent in a given year.

The human resources component was also important because universities are knowledge industries where people need to feel supported, empowered, and independent (but not overly independent) so that true learning occurs. But if I overdid it there, nothing would ever get done. As I said earlier, if all an institution does is serve its membership, over time it will have a difficult time surviving. Generally, people want to feel engaged in a larger purpose. On an annual basis, I gave the human resources component 25 percent. If one fails in this area, morale gets so low that nothing gets done.

Finally, the structural frame got 20 percent. The place must be well managed, and a larger vision is required. The ship must run efficiently and effectively, while making room for the creativity of others. This frame got less time because I have found that if the right people are in the right positions, and they are held accountable, things will get done.

Just for fun, I canvassed a dozen colleagues at major universities and a like number of business leaders. I asked them how much time they gave to each frame in their work. Because the group wasn't randomly picked and the number was small, it would be dangerous to generalize from their responses. However, I do feel comfortable making a few observations:

Both groups place a high value on the human resources frame, an average (mean) of 30 percent of their time devoted to this frame. There were several scores above 40 and just two below 15. No matter what we do, we can't ignore our people.

There was far greater variability with both the political and the symbolic frames, and the overall weights given were less than for the human resources or structural frames (18 was the average percentage for the political frame and 20 for the symbolic). As is true for all the frames, there is no real difference in the responses from either group. Since I know all of these people well, I can report that higher political scores came from business leaders, whose businesses required them to be "politically wired" to get contracts. The highest political scores for university presidents came from those in highly politicized states or who choose to spend their time in this way. The lowest score (10 percent) came from a college president who said he knew it was important but didn't like doing it; he assigned a very high-level person to represent him—a good example of self-awareness. For the symbolic frame, the range was from 5 percent to 40 percent. The lowest score came from a business leader who was solely responsible for production; marketing was done elsewhere. The highest score came from a private university president whose institution greatly depends on alumni and other private support.

The structural frame (average of 32 percent), received far greater emphasis than I gave it. There were five scores above 35 and a like number below 20. Although the average score was higher than the human resources frame, there was far greater variability. The highest business score came from a production-oriented company. But how to explain the several university presidents who reported scores of over 40? I think it is both a matter of personal style and interest, and, perhaps, an institutional need at a particular point in time.

So, what is to be gained from this discussion? Here's what I believe you can take home:

1. Different situations require different leadership styles.

2. The most successful situations occur when style and organizational or group needs coincide.

3. Most situations require more than one frame—and some require all. However, each situation will be weighted differently.

4. Most of us have more than one style. However, we're probably better at

some than others. Knowing our strengths and weaknesses, our predilections, is very important.

5. Our personality does influence how we weight the frames and how we delegate responsibility.

Reality Exercise. Think about a leadership situation in which you have been involved or which you have observed. Describe the situation and then describe which frame best explains the leadership approach used. As I did in my example, if there is more than one frame, assign a weight to the ones used, knowing that 100 percent is all you get.

Self-Awareness Exercise. Now describe yourself in relation to the four leadership frames. Which ones best describe you?

3

Self-Awareness and Emotional Competence

People become leaders for many reasons, but a stable sense of identity is likely to be found in all leaders.
> —Donald D. Clifton, "Signature Themes of Leadership," *Cutting Edge: Leadership* 2000

How do you identify the successful leader? The first thing I look for is emotional intelligence. Basically, how self-reflective is the person? Also it involves the teddy bear factor: do people feel comfortable with you?
> —Daniel Goleman, *Primal Leadership*

The realization of strengths and weaknesses is essential to growth as a leader.
> —Daniel Goleman, *Primal Leadership*

Let's go back to the title of this book: The Intentional Leader. Let's also remember its purpose: to help develop your leadership understanding and skills. This chapter will focus on you, describing some of the emotional characteristics that leaders have and then relating them to you. You also will be encouraged to use exercises to begin to better understand yourself and to continue to grow.

If you remember one thing from this chapter (but I expect you to remem-

ber much more), it should be the importance of self-awareness. Without self-awareness, it is difficult to master leadership. Here we are talking about emotional intelligence. Daniel Goleman,[1] who has worked with people in hundreds of companies worldwide, concludes that emotional intelligence is the most important factor in success at work and in life. In corporate matters, emotional intelligence plays an increasingly important role the higher up you go. Says Goleman: "the higher the rank of a person considered to be a star performer, the more emotional intelligence capability showed up as the reason for his or her effectiveness. . . . When I compared star performers with average ones in senior leadership positions, nearly 90 percent of the difference in their profiles was attributable to emotional intelligence factors rather than cognitive abilities."

This doesn't mean that intelligence is unimportant; we can assume that

1. Goleman, Boyatzis, and McKee, *Primal Leadership.*

most people in top positions, and in many other leadership situations, are above average in intelligence. Certainly having a higher IQ helps; but at some point, emotional intelligence kicks in as a way of distinguishing effective leaders from those who simply can't do it.

Shaw's Nine Components of Emotional Competence

I've observed nine components that help define our emotional competence or emotional intelligence. With a nod to the Menninger Foundation, here they are, followed by comments from other observers.

Ability to deal constructively with reality. The opposite of this ability is called denial, a defense mechanism that we use to shield ourselves from truth. Unfortunately, because we all have a need to cling to the familiar and safe, we don't go looking for bad news—even if it could save us. We'll do anything we can to make things seem okay. It's not easy, but it's essential that we avoid this trap, whether it is about our situation or ourselves. Effective leaders find ways to see things as they are.

Ability to adapt to change. None of us has the luxury of resisting change; it will occur with or without us. But leaders, in particular, must be willing to accommodate change and to help others make necessary transitions. This must be so in both the leaders' professional and personal lives. No, leaders don't jump on every bandwagon. But they are open to new ideas, evaluate them critically, induce a jolt of reality, and, when necessary, work for personal change. And they try to do the same for their organizations or groups.

Relative freedom from excessive anxiety or tension. All of us are anxious or tense at times; we live in a stressful world. But if we're stressed all the time, and new and difficult challenges result in our coming close to falling apart, it will be difficult for us to lead others. Constituents will quickly note the tension in the air; they'll avoid us rather than look to us for guidance.

There are pleasures associated with being a leader. As Chancellor of Syracuse University, I received a great deal of recognition. But it also gave me great pleasure to see initiatives pan out and things get better. I could become excited about the influence I believe I had over events—even feeling some exhilaration after successfully navigating conflict and danger. The perquisites of leadership are well understood, but the downside is the tension, the anxiety, and the stress that situations bring. As one guru said, "Leadership involves plumbing as well as poetry."[2] If the plumbing causes us too much pain, better let someone else do leadership.

Ability to find satisfaction in both giving and receiving. As children, we had to be taught the joys of giving to others. Eventually, most of us become mature enough to gain genuine satisfaction from giving to and helping others. We complete the maturity cycle when we're comfortable receiving something—help, a gift, or a compliment. Children pass through a stage of helplessness, to wanting to "do it myself," to being able to help others. The final measure of maturity is recognizing that we can't do everything ourselves and feeling at ease when we receive help.

Ability to form and maintain close relationships. As you will learn later, the leader must maintain some distance to keep his position in the group. Yet being open and honest with others—about issues, ways of doing things, and results—is essential. That doesn't mean making public your life's history. But you must have in your life someone you can trust, to whom you can risk exposing your doubts and fears. If you are unable to be close to anyone, you will lack the essential humanness that good leaders possess.

Wisdom to differentiate between the impossible and the possible. The concept, embraced by Alcoholics Anonymous in the Serenity Prayer, asks for acceptance of things that one cannot change, the courage to change the things one can, and the wisdom to know the difference. Effective leaders push the envelope in moving forward, but they don't select tasks that are impossible to accomplish. Having a goal that we'll all have to work very hard to achieve is better than having one that everyone knows won't happen.

Skill to redirect hostile energy into constructive outlets. Events don't give us problems, but our reactions to them do, say many clinical psychologists. Anger, for example, is normal and even healthy when it motivates us to make necessary changes. But constant anger drains us and those around us. Effective leaders find ways to redirect, rather than suppress, their negative feelings in various ways, including exercise, reading fiction, or such creative activities as writing or music.

Ability to love yourself and to love others. And we go back to self-awareness,

2. Daniel Goleman, "What Makes a Leader?" *Harvard Business Review*, Jan. 2004, 82–91.

because to truly love yourself you have to know yourself. If you really don't love yourself, it's very difficult for you to care for others; you're simply too needy yourself and too self-absorbed. In my capacity as a leader in various guises, I found myself subjected to what I call the fame/shame syndrome. I've been praised for accomplishments that weren't mine and damned for mistakes that I didn't make. As I moved up the higher education ladder, I found that my jokes were funnier and the venom in editorials castigating me much more bitter. Had I not had a good sense of myself and a capacity to love that self, warts and all, I could have been badly misled by external events.

Willingness to self-evaluate. We're back to self-awareness. Those of us who grow as leaders develop a capacity for hearing criticism and evaluating its truth and worth. Not everything that's offered to us is valid, but knowing what is requires an ability to be introspective and self-correcting.

Let me make you feel better now. No leader has all these qualities nailed down. Some are very strong in one area but struggle with others. Some leaders are lovable hotheads who seem able to blow their stacks once in a while but compensate in other ways. Others have a hard time managing their anxiety but work through it and are quick to empathize with others, helping to move on the agenda. Later, in our exercises, you'll be asked to reflect on what all this means to you.

Daniel Goleman's Five Components of Emotional Intelligence

Let's now turn to the master, Daniel Goleman,[3] who believes that emotional intelligence can be developed. He lists five components of emotional intelligence: self-awareness, self-regulation, motivation, empathy, and social skill.

Self-awareness. It is essential to becoming emotionally intelligent. Self-aware people appear self-confident, can realistically assess themselves, and have a good sense of humor—they are willing to laugh when the joke's on them.

Self-regulation. Goleman says we can't do away with the biological impulses that drive our emotions, but we must learn to manage them. This allows us to be freed from the prison of our own feelings—not to give way to bad

3. Goleman, "What Makes a Leader?"

> "Self-aware leaders are tuned to their inner signals. If a person is perpetually oblivious to his own feelings, he will also be tuned out to how others feel."
>
> —Daniel Goleman, *Primal Leadership*

moods and emotional impulses, but to control and even channel them in useful ways. He believes this is necessary because people who can control their feelings and impulses can better create an environment of trust. "No one wants to be known as a hothead when the boss is known for her calm approach. Fewer bad moods at the top mean fewer throughout the organization." Hallmarks of self-regulated leaders are their trustworthiness and integrity, their comfort with ambiguous situations, and their openness to change.

Motivation. Here the key word, Goleman says, is *achieve.* Plenty of people are motivated by external factors such as salary or status, but motivated leaders are driven to achieve simply for the sake of achievement. They have the physical and emotional energy to pursue goals with great persistence and a strong optimism even in the face of failure. They never give up.

Empathy. This is the ability to understand and consider another person's feelings. That doesn't mean being so caught up in their problems that you can't objectively lead. Goleman cites an example of empathy in action. Imagine two giant brokerage companies merging, creating redundant jobs in the new organization. One division manager calls his people together and gives a gloomy speech that emphasized the number of people who would soon be fired. The manager of another division gives his people a different kind of speech. He is upfront about his own worry and confusion, and he promises to keep people informed and to treat everyone fairly. The difference between the two managers is empathy. The first manager was too worried about his own fate, Goleman states, to consider the feelings of his colleagues. The second knew what others were feeling and he acknowledged his fears and theirs. Empathy is important, Goleman believes, because of the increasing use of work teams.

Social skill. Like empathy, social skill involves a person's ability to manage relationships. Social skill, Goleman believes, is "friendliness with a purpose: moving people in the direction you desire whether that's agreement on a new marketing strategy or enthusiasm about a new product. Socially skilled people tend to have a wide circle of acquaintances, and they have a knack for finding common ground with people of all kinds—a knack for building rapport."

Goleman leaves us with a sense of optimism because he believes that emotional intelligence can be developed. It may be difficult, but it is worth the effort.

Qualities of Leaders: An International View

Finally, here's just one more way of looking at leadership qualities. Robert J. House and colleagues[4] have conducted a ten-year research program studying sixty-two different societies and their views about leadership. Although cultural differences play a role in leadership—and we'll get to them later—they report a fairly long list of leadership attributes universally endorsed by respondents in their sixty-two-society sample. They are the positive attributes of being:

- Trustworthy, just, and honest (integrity)
- Foresighted and able to plan ahead
- Positive, dynamic, encouraging, motivating, and able to build confidence
- Communicative, informed, a coordinator, and a team builder

They also found some common negative attributes. They described ineffective leaders as loners, asocial, uncooperative, irritable, nonexplicit, egocentric, ruthless, and dictatorial.

You can see similarities in my observations, the work of Daniel Goleman, and the intercultural studies of House et al. Chief among them is that leaders need to be emotionally intelligent and well grounded. Let's turn now to ways that you can begin to better understand yourself and develop approaches for improving your performance in areas of your choice.

Making It Work for You

Are you surprised to hear that self-assessment comes first? What's to improve if you don't know enough about yourself to get started? So, in this chapter and

4. Robert House et al., eds., *Culture Leadership and Organizations: The GLOBE Study of 62 Countries* (Thousand Oaks, Calif.: Sage, 2004).

later, you are asked to take a good look at yourself in a variety of areas, to compare what you see with the observations of someone who knows you well, and to determine where your strengths, weaknesses, interests, and noninterests lie.

After self-awareness comes the development of a plan for improvement in areas you select. After the plan must come action. Goleman[5] gives an excellent example. Let's say you've determined that you want to improve your ability as a speaker, keeping in mind that we earlier learned that communication is essential for leadership. Having established that you need to improve, you then make a plan. Goleman gives this example of such a plan:

• Give at least two formal presentations every month, and have them critiqued by a peer I respect.

• Practice with a friend before giving a presentation.

• Videotape myself giving a speech and critique it with the help of others.

• Join Toastmasters so I can practice giving more effective talks.

• Talk to people who give oral presentations in a manner that comes across as relaxed and interesting, and find out what they do to prepare — specifically, how they overcome stage fright and relax during the presentation.

Now, there's a plan. It is specific and doable. It then, of course, requires more: Do it. Carry it out. Practice. Analyze how things went. Determine what more must be done.

The Goleman illustration is a good example of how you can improve your speaking. Let's look at some others. The best three-point shooters in college basketball have a great deal of talent. But they also practice, and in doing so they simulate game conditions. These aren't just idle shots thrown up past the three-point line. Each one is purposeful. Michael Jordan had a great deal of natural ability, but he practiced harder and more purposefully than anyone else. He became a great shot by shooting purposefully in practice. You can't expect to change old habits simply by learning new ones and developing a plan. The practice must be intense. If a piano player takes hours to learn a small piece of music, why would you think you can change a given behavior in less time and with less effort? Practice — repetition — more practice — more repetition; this is the key to strengthening certain behaviors.

And don't overlook mental rehearsal. I've often found that mental re-

5. Goleman, Boyatzis, and McKee, *Primal Leadership*, 149.

hearsal is extremely helpful in preparing for something important or in attempting to strengthen an area. Athletes have known this for decades. While practice is essential, mental rehearsal can greatly influence one's effectiveness. As mentioned earlier, I once got hooked into a one-mile race against several contemporaries. Not particularly fast or agile, I trained for several months hoping to get my track practice time below six minutes, which for me, a fair athlete but no runner, would be no easy feat. In chapter 1, I described my practice routine. But mental rehearsal also led to a major improvement in performance. Each night, before running my practice mile or other distances, I rehearsed each step of the laps around the track. I forced myself to think about the wind, the feelings in my legs (tired), and what I needed to do to pick up the pace. By the day of the race, I did little but visualize what the event was going to be like—each step of the way. My time was 5:52, for me a world-beater. I won the race, and I learned a far more important lesson: a technique that has stayed with me in preparing for big meetings, for speeches, and in strengthening skill areas that needed work.

So, understanding your strengths and weaknesses, having a plan, and carrying it out—the whole package—are how you achieve self-improvement. Practice! Practice! Practice! Let's try some exercises.

Self-Awareness Exercises. Let's move on to the leader in you. Steve and John Simmons[6] have developed ways to measure emotional intelligence. These tests are used both for individuals for self-assessment and by employers for hiring and developing employees. On one test, the Simmonses ask test takers to rate themselves on thirteen factors:

1. Slow paced/fast paced
2. Relaxed/stressed
3. Faultfinding/positive
4. Humble/self-assured
5. Leisurely/hardworking

---

6. Steve Simmons and John C. Simmons, Jr., *Measuring Emotional Intelligence: Groundbreaking Guide to Applying the Principles of Emotional Intelligence* (Arlington, Tex.: Summit, 1997).

6. Spontaneous/careful
7. Routine/challenging
8. Cautious/courageous
9. Hesitant/decisive
10. Compliant/assertive
11. Intolerant/tolerant
12. Self-willed/considerate
13. Reserved/sociable

There are no right answers; but you might better understand yourself if you think about yourself in each of these areas. For each, determine which best describes you. For example, do you tend to be slow-paced, sort of in the middle, or fast-paced? Are you usually relaxed, sort of in the middle, or usually highly stressed? From that exercise, write up a brief description of yourself as seen by you. Now have a friend or colleague do the same, describing you as she sees you. Then compare your assessment to hers.

Here's another way of looking at yourself. Lussier and Achua[7] have a self-assessment exercise that helps to determine your interest in and readiness for leadership. Again, there are no right or wrong answers, but it gives you a sense of how you really feel about things.

1. Are you interested in and willing to take charge of a group of people, or would you rather have someone else do it?

2. When you're not in charge, are you still willing to give input, or do you hold back your suggestions?

3. Do you enjoy trying to influence people to your point of view, or would you rather not be bothered?

4. When you're in charge of an activity, do you want to delegate some of the responsibility, or do you end up doing it all?

5. Do you like to work with people and see them succeed, or is that of little interest to you?

6. Do you like having clear goals and working with others to see them realized, or would you really prefer to take things as they come?

7. Robert N. Lussier and Christopher F. Achua, *Leadership: Theory Application, Skill Development* ([Mason, Ohio]: Thompson/South-Western, 2004).

7. Do you like to do and learn new things, or would you rather keep things pretty much as they are?

Reality Exercise. Enough self-analysis. From what you have read in the section, you should have identified at least some of your strengths and weaknesses, as well as your interests. Jot down one weakness you would really like to address. Then develop a plan, as suggested by Goleman. The next step will be carrying it out. Practice to get better, and practice to evaluate how you are doing. Practice to determine if any adjustments are necessary. Plan *and* practice. You can do it if you commit. And leaders commit.

What Does Terry Say?
(Terry is a middle management executive in an international consulting firm)

Terry, what are the three most significant characteristics of outstanding leaders you have worked with?

1. They show they care about getting the job done and about me. They put the time in themselves and they're willing to listen to different viewpoints. Whether they accept my ideas is less important than their caring about my opinion and their wanting us to do our best.

2. They see the big picture. They know there are many pieces to the puzzle but they don't bog us down on the little pieces.

3. By their actions, they demonstrate honesty and integrity and respect for others.

Terry, what are the three most significant characteristics of the ineffective leaders you've been around?

1. They have a short-term perspective about their work, viewing it mainly as a way to advance themselves rather than to improve the organization or achieve its purposes.

2. They tend to be arbitrary and noncommunicative.

3. They can't stay on course, continually changing their minds.

4

Skills for Effective Leadership

Up to here, you've learned what leaders do and their common characteristics. You've tried on this information to see how it fits. Now it's time to look at tools that can make you more effective. We'll work with a number of skills, all designed to help you get people to join you in a good cause. You'll learn about conflict and how to resolve it. Motivational tools will follow, as well as learning to use your leadership power constructively and ethically.

In this chapter, you also will learn effective decision-making and communication techniques and how to deal with crises. Where practical, you will be given some "think" and "do" assignments to help you use and get comfortable with the skills we will be discussing.

Conflict Resolution

As frequently as we're involved in conflict situations, we receive remarkably little guidance about handling them. Conflict is the order of the day in our kind of society and, as you will learn, it is often essential for its advancement. Psychologists tell us that the potential for conflict exists in every human and animal society because of competition for resources and, for humans, disagreements over courses of action. Most human conflicts, however, are not violent, although nonproductive verbal exchanges often occur. Before we begin learning about conflict, here's a brief test.

Komives[1] provides a framework for thinking about conflict resolution. I've repeated it below so that you can think about your personal style in deal-

1. Komives, Lucas, and McMahon, *Exploring Leadership.*

ing with conflict situations. Read the descriptions that are contained below and assign a percentage to each conflict style based on how often you use it when you get into conflict situations. You get 100 points.

Style 1: I avoid conflict and stay away from issues involving conflict.

Style 2: I want to be the winner in conflict situations.

Style 3: I want to be liked, so I avoid conflict.

Style 4: I believe in compromise.

Style 5: I view conflict as an opportunity to identify and solve problems.

Write down your answers to these five descriptors, and keep them handy. After you've read and worked through the chapter, you will be asked to do it again to spot any differences in your responses.

First, let me allay your fears. Conflict is inevitable, so you might as well face up to it. It's not necessarily your fault nor does it mean the other person is bad. If you find yourself in conflict situations, it only means you're human; it doesn't mean something's wrong with you. Something's wrong only if you aren't using these situations productively. In many cases, conflict is a constructive force, to be exploited for improving a personal or group situation.

Social institutions often thrive and advance on conflict. Without it, we would stagnate. In the British film "The Third Man," spy Harry Lime, played by Orson Welles, wryly notes that decades of warfare and bloodshed in medieval Europe produced the Renaissance, and five hundred years of peace and brotherly love in Switzerland produced the cuckoo clock. Of course this is hyperbole, but it underscores my point: conflict is a certainty, and we can use it for constructive change. Doing otherwise is to let conflict control us.

Knowing that conflict isn't always your fault is also good for your mental health.

Approaches to Conflict

In Western culture, conflict can take one of three courses—aside from all-out war or other violence.

The collegial model. In this model, opposing opinions fortunately are accompanied by a common goal or goals. The parties try to reach an agreement and, in theory, that agreement provides a better solution than anyone could have reached alone. This is called a creative shift: a group working together finds a solution better than anything they had individually imagined. Here is a simple illustration: three people bitterly want the one orange left in the refrigerator. They discuss the wisdom of dividing it into three equal pieces, flipping coins, fighting, or whatever. But as they discuss their separate goals, they find that Mary wants to use the pulp for juice, Joe wants to use the rind for an art project, and Bill, living in upstate New York, wants to use the seeds to plant an orange tree. Isn't this wonderful? Their solution made them all happy.

I haven't seen too many faculty committees work this way. Nor have I often seen groups in business come up with such collegial solutions. If you believe that every conflict encounter must end this way, you'll be unhappy most of the time. And if you tell me that your conflicts always end this way and convince me of that, you could make a fortune selling cuckoo clocks. I'll buy one from you.

The collegial model is what we all hope and strive for, but it's naïve to assume conflict always will end this way. It's certainly worth trying, though.

The zero-sum model. In this model, such a hard line is taken that one side must win and the other lose, as in football or chess. Fisher and Ury[2] call this hard bargaining.

We usually have two outcomes in mind when we engage in a conflict. First, we want to reach an agreement that meets our needs and our goals. Second, we want to maintain an appropriate relationship with the other person. If that relationship is ongoing, an agreement satisfying to everyone is all the more important. A zero-sum solution leaves little room for working constructively together in the future. Such resolutions usually leave one side very unhappy. To paraphrase Machiavelli, unless you can destroy someone, don't go around ticking him off.

In your personal and professional lives, you are in great danger if you feel your conflicts must all be resolved through the zero-sum model — especially if you think you must win them all. (Although if you feel you must lose them all you're not going to do well, either.) If your conflicts always are resolved to your advantage, and they are zero-sum situations, I guarantee that you'll have a lot of angry people around you, and if you're married, you'd better get a good

---

2. Roger Fisher and William Ury, *Getting to Yes: Negotiating Agreement Without Giving In* (New York: Penguin Books, 1981).

lawyer. On the other hand, if you've never had a zero-sum situation, then you probably have compromised issues to no one's betterment. It shows you are unwilling to make hard choices.

Solomon-like solutions—cutting the baby in half—don't work in every case. The challenge is to determine when conflicts are zero-sum situations and when they are not.

For me, the termination of employees always is a difficult, zero-sum solution. But if they can't or won't respond to my efforts to help them improve and get with the program, they have to go. There's no effective compromise here.

Also, when we find ourselves having to allocate resources, surrendering to the temptation to give everyone the same may not be best for the organization. For example, when major cuts must be made at a university, perhaps closing a school or college is better than weakening the overall enterprise.

Remember self-awareness from chapter 2; it is vital that you understand and deal with your own motives in such situations. Are you working toward an acceptable agreement or battling for a zero-sum solution to fulfill some ego needs that you'd rather not confront?

In short, zero-sum conflicts sometimes must occur. If they occur too often, your leadership ability will be extremely compromised.

Reality Exercise. Think a minute about situations you've seen involving zero-sum solutions to conflicts. Which ones were the correct solutions and which ones were not?

Strategic negotiation model. This is in many ways the labor relations model, and it works in most conflicts. In it, both sides find it advantageous to yield somewhat, with the outcome being a negotiated compromise. Most conflicts take this course, which is in the American tradition of organized labor, shared governance in universities, and most business and not-for-profit situations.

Strategic negotiation requires that we're willing to concede some points, hold firm where we must, and work toward a resolution where the overall goals are best achieved.

It means keeping your eye on the target—knowing your goals. It means downplaying your personal and ego needs. Fisher and Ury believe that negotiations may be fairly judged by three criteria: the agreement should: (1) be wise, (2) be efficient, and (3) improve, or at least not damage, our relationships with each other.

To "get to yes," they recommend separating the people from the problem. It's the problem you're trying to work out; it's not the good guys against the bad guys. They advocate focusing on interests versus positions, where a variety of positions could satisfy a given interest. They suggest generating a variety of possibilities before deciding or agreeing on what to do and insist that results be based on some objective standard. Finally, they see assuming a fixed pie or searching for a single answer as far too limiting in trying to negotiate a fair agreement. Strategic negotiation is hard work, but it is necessary to reach an acceptable agreement.

> *Reality Exercise.* Think of several recent conflict situations you have been involved in or have observed. They can be personal, work, or volunteer. Describe the situation and the outcome. Which of the three models were applied in each case? Were there successful outcomes? What was it about the process and the outcome that made it successful? Were there any unsuccessful outcomes? Why were they unsuccessful?

Conflict Resolution Techniques

I've described these three outcomes to help you think about how to deal with the fluid situations that come up in conflict resolution. That's the first step. The second is to develop conflict resolution techniques so that you can heavily influence a final outcome and keep relationships intact.

The techniques I describe will be valuable to you personally. But unlike with some skills you develop, you're better off if the opposing parties are aware of them, too. The more people know about how to resolve differences, the better off everyone is. I'm giving you a wonderful gift to share with others. You will find these skills easy to remember, a little more difficult to imagine how to use, and very difficult to do—unless you practice. Using the following techniques in the sequence presented can enhance successful resolution of conflict.

Listen. This is a skill few of us have. One person has said that a good listener is a talker with a sore throat. Or, as another wrote, "God gave us two ears but only one mouth. Some say that's because he/she wanted us to spend twice as much time listening as talking. Others say it is because listening is twice as hard as talking!"

Listening is more difficult than talking, but it is a skill that can be mastered. When we listen, we receive information and learn what is truly important to the other party. If you're truly listening, and you convey that to your antagonist, he can relax, and you can both deal with issues rather than personalities.

Listening allows us to focus on solutions. The importance of silence can't be underestimated. Get your watch out—don't say anything for thirty seconds. Notice how long that seemed. In our conversations with others, we seem bent on avoiding these uncomfortable silences. What's wrong with a thirty- or sixty-second silence? If we don't allow for silences, we simply take turns trying to fill the void. Or we both try to talk at the same time. Either way we're talking past one another. If the other party has difficulty with silences (the most important clue is interrupting), you can talk about the importance of silence as you work toward a solution. Remember, you're not trying to make points; you're trying to get to a positive resolution of your disagreement.

Listening also involves watching body language, such as eye contact and arm movement. Often, body language tells you what the person really wants you to know, as will changes in her voice.

Here is a listening exercise. Have someone read it to you, and truly listen to what is being said:

> I'm really angry at you. You've been subverting me since the beginning of this project—one that requires a great deal of cooperation. You and your people disagree with everything I advance. We're here to improve productivity by 50 percent. To me that means large staff cuts. It also means we're going to have to take on more work. You and your people need to get with the program.

Did you hear what the person said? While you might not have liked it, it's important that you heard it.

Repeat in your own words what has been said. This ensures that you correctly understand the other party's positions. There's no better way to show that you are really listening, that you care about his opinions, and that you want to work things out. It's how you say, "I'm listening." Now let's go back to the above statement. Have someone read it to you, and think about your response.

Here is my response:

> So you don't think that I've been cooperative. This obviously makes you angry. You believe that because I don't agree with suggestions you've made that I'm subverting your efforts. You want to improve productivity, and to you it means that we have to cut staff and take on more work. Is that what you're telling me?

You don't need to do this for the whole conversation, but better to err on the side of overuse than underuse. I'm not concerned that you'll overuse it.

Indicate areas of agreement with the other person's position. This will eliminate subjects you don't have to discuss because you've already reached agreement on them. Noncontentious issues can be set aside. For example, if there are ten issues for discussion, and you discover that you agree to seven, you've already made good progress, and there's more reason for a buy in. This greatly reduces tension.

I've seen it work and have often used flipcharts outlining the areas of agreement. The parties involved see that the need for overall agreement is important and that they're off to a good start. They see that there is much advantage to be realized by resolving some or all of the remaining differences. "We are almost there!"

Now here's my effort to indicate agreement:

> I fully agree that we need to work together to improve productivity. Management requires it, and our overall viability—our jobs—require that we see enormous improvement. I also agree that it will mean some staff cuts, taking on more work, and I want to work together with you in fleshing out the bones so that we can have an effective plan to present to management, one that will get the job done.

What Does Terry Say?

I had a conflict once where we spent a great deal of time arguing—then finally got down to work. It was over the sales people wanting to have a product up and running in three weeks in order to close the sale. Those in operations and engineering were saying it couldn't be done in less than six weeks. We got very heated. We eventually calmed down but could reach no resolution. We agreed to kick it upstairs to our respective bosses. My boss in sales called his opposite and asked this question, "What would it take for you to be able to do it in three weeks?" His partner told him what kinds of resources would be needed, but said even with those resources it would take four weeks not three. The two agreed to ask the president for those resources so that the job could be done in four weeks. We got the contract and the job got done. I should have asked the other side, "What will it take for you to get the job done in three weeks?" But at least we got a workable decision.

Then, and only then, indicate areas of disagreement. Now is the time to reconcile those differences. So far, you've listened, shown that you understand what the person was saying, and indicated where you share similar views. You've agreed on a number of items, and now it's time to get down to what is left. Let's go back to the original statement. I would repeat what the person said and indicate my areas of agreement. Then I would say,

I'm not sure that our staff needs to be slashed drastically, but I'm willing to discuss it. We should put other options on the table. We might consider cutting everyone's salary temporarily. We might look at some creative situations to resolve the issues—bringing in marketing to increase sales and finding ways to improve the product so that we can solve part of our problem on the revenue side. I would hope that our discussions would involve looking at any number of options that either of us can put on the table.

Also, I don't agree that my disagreeing with you means I'm subverting you and your group. Let's agree that we will have differences of opinion and try to work through them. I don't see much gained by our believing that disagreement means disloyalty.

Is this okay with you?

As I mentioned earlier, the four steps aren't that hard to remember, and maybe a little harder to imagine using, but it becomes far more difficult actually to use them, and that will take much practice. Practice!

In summary, you've learned the three outcomes of conflict: collegial, zero-sum, and strategic. You've also learned that conflict is inevitable and that you avoid it only at your risk. Finally, I've shown you that four simple steps can resolve many differences. They are: (1) listening, (2) repeating, (3) indicating areas of agreement, and, then and only then, (4) indicating areas of disagreement.

To sharpen your understandings and skills, here are some practice assignments.

Self-Awareness Exercise. Think of a conflict situation that you've recently confronted. Using what you've just learned, describe how it was resolved. What outcome (collegial, zero-sum, or strategic) occurred? Were any of the skills you've learned used? How could it have been done better?

Reality Exercise. Now let's move from a simple exercise to some practice. Find a way to practice the four-step plan at least five times a week. You don't need a conflict situation to master listening, repeating, and agreeing. Keep practicing until you feel a comfort level. You'll also find that there are enough conflict situations where you'll be able to use all four.

At first, you'll feel uncomfortable but as your comfort level increases you'll get better. Try lighter situations such as deciding what movie to go to or what to have for dinner, but work at using these techniques. Keep doing them, and keep track of how you're doing. Also, reflect on what's working for you and what's not. Remember, practice will do the trick.

Now, let's consider the five questions we originally asked about conflict style. Answer them again without looking at your initial answers. Here's the exercise again:

Read the descriptions that are contained below and assign a percentage to each conflict style based on how often you use it when you get into conflict situations. You get 100 points.

Style 1: I avoid conflict and stay away from issues involving conflict.

Style 2: I want to be the winner in conflict situations.

Style 3: I want to be liked, so I avoid conflict.

Style 4: I believe in compromise.

Style 5: I view conflict as an opportunity to identify and solve problems.

Now look at your first answers and compare the two. Are they different? How? If they're not different, decide if you're comfortable with where you presently are in your understanding of yourself vis-à-vis conflict.

Motivating Others

> *Leaders attract followers — because of their deep respect of the aspirations of others.*
> — James M. Kouzes and Barry Z. Posner, *The Leadership Challenge*

> *No major venture will succeed without highly motivated men and women.*
> — John Gardner, *On Leadership*

> *A leader must recognize the needs of followers or constituents and help them see how these needs can be met and give them the confidence that they can accomplish that result through their efforts.*
> — Anonymous

To lead, you must motivate. We'll start learning how to get others to buy in by examining the complexity of motivation. Then I will give you some simple hints about the best way to approach motivating others.

Complexity

First, the complexity. Herzberg,[3] through his research, has observed that motivating isn't as easy as it sounds. The things that make people satisfied and motivated in their jobs are different in kind from the things that make them dissatisfied. "The opposite of job satisfaction is not job dissatisfaction but, rather, *no job satisfaction*; and similarly the opposite of job dissatisfaction is not job satisfaction but *no job dissatisfaction*." Herzberg is saying that many of the extrinsic motivators simply don't work. Eliminating some of the sources of dissatisfaction doesn't necessarily motivate people to do more and better on the job. As much as you'll hear about an annoying boss, low salary, uncom-

---

3. Frederick Herzburg, "One More Time: How to Motivate Employees," *Harvard Business Review*, Jan. 2003, 3–11.

fortable workspace, or stupid rules, the elimination of these problems doesn't automatically lead to improved performance. Herzberg names some of what he calls hygiene factors. They are:

Reducing time spent at work. Not a good idea he says. Actually, the Germans and the French are finding that they can't be economically competitive with their highly vaunted thirty-five-hour work week. In many parts of Germany and France, it is now being raised back to forty hours.

Increasing wages, increasing fringe benefits, improved communications, etc. It's not that these things are unimportant and not the right thing to do. They just aren't highly motivating over the long run.

Herzberg believes that the best way to motivate people is to make their jobs more enriching. Here is how he proposes to do this:

• Increase individuals' accountability for their work by removing some controls.

• Give people responsibility for a complete process or a unit of work.

• Make information available directly to employees rather than sending it through their managers first.

• Enable people to take on new, more difficult tasks that they haven't handled before.

• Assign individuals specialized tasks that allow them to become experts.

The payoff, he says, is employees who gain an enhanced sense of responsibility and achievement, along with new opportunities to learn and grow continually.

The Forum for College and University Governance offers a similar point of view.[4] It describes the dilemma of motivating knowledge workers, an increasingly large portion of our workforce: "[M]ost employees believe that they are above average performers and therefore are entitled to some of the rewards earmarked for merit." One study was telling: 90 percent of blue collar and professional respondents rated themselves as above average in performance. In yet another study, almost half of the employees surveyed placed themselves in the top 5 percent in the quality of their work. Midwestern comic and sage Garrison Keillor apparently was right about the people of Lake Wobegon: "Here

4. "Incentives and Knowledge Workers: Oil and Water?" from *Briefings*, the newsletter of the Forum for College and University Governance, Univ. of Maryland, 1989, 4.

the women are strong, the men are good looking, and all of the children are above average." It describes many work situations today.

So, motivating others is not easy. Here's the first important take-home point: *people are subject to a variety of motivating influences, and no one size fits all.* Further, the culture of the workplace and other organizational settings very much affect which motivators will work. So, while one size won't fit all, try what's below on for size.

Human Exchange: It Has Worked since the Beginning of Time

In an earlier life, I had a very close friend whose name was Sam. Sam was an extremely effective state senator. At one of our lunches, I could see that I didn't have his undivided attention — he was writing in a little black book. I asked him what he was doing; he apologized and said that he had just thought of a favor that he had done for another person and wanted to write it down so that he had the record and could call in "chits" at a future time. He worked hard to achieve a 50–50 ratio of favors received to favors given. That is exchange!

That might turn you off, but in truth, the various currencies we use in our interactions with people do motivate them, and human exchange occurs in just about everything we do. Stephen Covey[5] put it another way. In our relationships with others, we build an emotional bank account that works about the same way as a financial bank account, where we make deposits and build up a reserve. He believes that this is what builds trust, with the most important deposits being courtesy, kindness, honesty, and keeping one's commitment. You build trust and you get things in return.

It isn't just about trust, because different currencies work for different people. Giving is not only right, moral, and satisfying, but this currency of human exchange is what works to get others to embrace you and your vision.

What currencies motivate people to want to do things? What can you give them, even if you're not their boss or in a position of power, to make them want to do things for you? Cohen and Bradford[6] effectively describe the various kinds of currencies we can use to motivate others (see fig. 1). Different sit-

5. Stephen R. Covey, *Principle-Centered Leadership* (New York: Summit, 1991).
6. Allan Cohen and David Bradford, *Influence Without Authority* (New York: John Wiley, 1990).

Figure 1. Currencies Frequently Valued in Organizations

Inspiration-Related Currencies

Vision	Being involved in a task that has larger significance for unit, organization, constituents, or society
Excellence	Having a chance to do important things really well
Moral/Ethical Correctness	Doing what is right by a higher standard than efficiency

Task-Related Currencies

New Resources	Obtaining money, budget increases, personnel, space, etc.
Challenge/Learning Assistance	Getting help with existing projects or unwanted tasks
Task Support	Receiving overt or subtle backing or actual assistance with implementation
Rapid Response	Quicker response time
Information	Access to organizational as well as technical knowledge

Position-Related Currencies

Recognition	Acknowledgment of effort, accomplishment, or abilities
Visibility	The chance to be known by higher-ups or significant others in the organization
Reputation	Being seen as competent, committed
Insider/Importance	A sense of belonging to inner circle
Contacts	Links to others

Relationship-Related Currencies

Understanding	Having concerns and issues listened to
Acceptance/Inclusion	Closeness and friendship
Personal Support	Personal and emotional backing

Personal-Related Currencies

Gratitude	Appreciation or expression of indebtedness
Ownership/Involvement	Ownership of and influence over important tasks
Self-Concept	Affirmation of one's values, self-esteem, and identity
Comfort	Avoidance of roadblocks and other hassles

Source: Allan R. Cohen and David L. Bradford, *Influence without Authority*, 1990. Reprinted by permission of John Wiley and Sons, New York.

uations require different currencies, and individuals and groups usually are motivated by more than one kind. There's no one perfect currency for anyone.

Inspiration-related currencies. Here you are inspiring people to a higher calling, asking them to be a part of something big, something important, something moral. Or you are inviting them to be actors in a wonderful drama and do important things well. These are inspirational currencies. There are people who will rise to extraordinary efforts if they believe in the vision, and vision is what makes them want to go far more than the extra mile. As Herzberg observes, motivated people aren't looking for fewer hours to work; rather they want to do *more.*

Task-related currencies. I once had an employee who would call me late at night (11 P.M. is late for me) seeking information. I discouraged late calls unless they were emergencies, but I always made an exception for this person. Why? Because he still was at the office working on a project; if I gave him the information he was seeking, he would have the job done by morning, which was extremely important to him (and to me). This is an example of someone who is motivated by task-related currencies. Thank God there are people who find great satisfaction in a job well done. They feel best when their report is finished. You'll be repaid many times over if you can offer them resources, relief from unwanted and unproductive tasks, support at a higher level, a quick response to their questions, and, always, a quick response to their need for information. Such people will follow you anywhere.

Position-related currencies. Many people thrive when they get recognition, their achievements are made visible, they are seen as competent and committed, and they are considered part of the inner circle. This currency works great for them, and if you play things right they will repay more than what you give them. Company recognition programs work well for them (although you will perhaps notice that some employees would rather not).

Relationship-related currencies. Some colleagues need to feel that they're very close to you. They need more of your time, and getting it is their reward for being highly motivated. Sometimes they need a sympathetic ear and personal support. Some can be brought to tears by a thank-you note or an expression of concern about a problem. Giving them time is very important, so your challenge is to be friendly and helpful but avoid being over-familiar, as the latter will reduce your overall influence over time. And you can't give them unlimited attention.

The mistakes made in not understanding the various currencies are legion. Let me recite a few. One of my colleagues believed in leading by inspiration alone. He made the best speeches of any college president; they were visionary and inspiring. While people listened with rapt attention, little was done, as the other currencies simply weren't there to motivate. His inspiring thoughts made for good reading but little advancement—there was no oomph to the vision. Another master of relationship currencies never missed a birthday celebration, memorial service, or an invitation to dinner. Everyone liked him but little got done; he was a one-currency man, discounted as nice but ineffectual.

Here's an example of putting this approach to work: you are a design person and are having difficulty working something out. You know Bill to be the most creative and analytical person in your organization, and you have no direct relationship to him. You get along okay, but how can you motivate him to give you some of his time?

First, if he's relationship oriented, you can work harder at being his friend, get to know him better, and spend some out-of-work time with him to build up those currencies. Perhaps you can appeal to his desire for the company to prosper and suggest that if his design materializes, everyone benefits. Or perhaps he needs recognition. Sell him on your willingness to give him much of the credit should this design become a winner. Or perhaps, knowing that he is task motivated, you could get your superior to provide additional resources so that he can devote his energies to your problem.

Here's another example: you're running the United Way fund drive and you need thousand of supporters. You start with a speech to the large group of people doing the much-needed leg work (perhaps having it teleconferenced), outlining the importance of the campaign and inspiring people to make this the best ever. You make sure initiatives are supported with necessary funding (important to the task-related people) and that early achievements are publicly rewarded and praised (for those who are motivated in this way). Individuals who have done outstanding work are recognized with personal thanks and public recognition. And during the campaign you spend "quality time" with a small number of loyal supporters who will be motivated by this currency.

Nothing works perfectly, but knowing these currencies and using them will help you motivate others.

> *Reality Exercise.* Identify six to eight coworkers or people you spend a lot of time with outside of a work. Identify which currencies work best for each person. Then visualize how you might use these currencies to move an agenda with them.

> *Self-Awareness Exercise.* You're made chairman of a nine-member work group in a large architectural firm. Your charge is to suggest several new options for the company logo. You didn't volunteer for this assignment, nor did your eight colleagues, all of whom are loyal to the company but are busy people. Think about how you would use the currencies to motivate them to help you get the job done.

The Power That Can Be Yours

> *The nice thing about being a celebrity is that when you bore people, they think it's their fault.*
> —Henry Kissinger

> *A spoiled child never loves its mother.*
> —Sir Henry Taylor

> *If absolute power corrupts absolutely, does absolute powerlessness make us pure?*
> —Some smart aleck

In the previous section, you've learned techniques for motivating others, to influence them to action. Now you will learn that understanding and ethically using your potential power can greatly strengthen your ability to move things. Briefly stated, power is "A's ability to move B to act"—in other words, to get people to do things you want them to do.

To some, power is an ugly word, connoting dominance or manipulation at the expense of someone else's self-esteem. That can be so. But make no mistake: the ability to control and influence others allows us to direct the agenda,

and it can be done ethically. Any tool or technique can be used for good or ill. Just because it can be used unethically doesn't mean you shouldn't use it ethically.

The word *power* usually conjures up the vision of people in high places sitting behind large desks making decisions about other people's lives. That's probably true, but it's only a small piece of the power dimension. In truth, as you will see, we all have power to influence others. Not all of us use that power, but it's there for our use. Peter Block believes that even the people at the top are in the middle; that there is no absolute power in an organization.[7]

So, those at the top have less power than you might imagine, and those in the middle and at the bottom of any hierarchy have far more power than they know. Again, Block tells us that many critical decisions are made by people much lower in the hierarchy.

7. Peter Block, *The Empowered Manager: Positive Skills and Work* (San Francisco: Jossey-Bass, 1987).

> "All good things can be misused except virtue." — Unknown

So, you will learn about using power as a tool, and how it can be done ethically. It is there for your taking, and if you don't, others will.

What motivates you to do something? McClelland and Burnham[8] believe that personal motivation is very important in leading. A key to success is the achievement motive—the desire to do something better or more efficiently than it has been done before. But, they say, there is more to our motivation than the need for achievement. They see the need for power and the use of power as essential tools for getting results. From their research they conclude that top leaders "must possess a high need for power." But, they maintain, this need must be disciplined and controlled so that it is directed toward the benefit of the institution (the cause) as a whole and not toward the personal agenda of the individual. They say that the need for power must be much stronger than the need for being liked. If our need for being liked is too great (affiliative managers), we can't get others to do their best since we expend too much of our effort on achieving their esteem. They sense that and give us what we want—but not results.

Obviously, the need for power can go too far. Leaders overly concerned with personal power tend to lack self-control and act impulsively or arbitrarily. "They are not good institutional builders," say McClelland and Burnham.

Sources of Power

So, effective leaders see power as an essential tool but use it to benefit the cause rather than their own personal needs. This is the ethical use of power.

Now let's turn to the sources of that power that can be yours. I give due credit to Jim Fisher,[9] a strong and successful leader, a good friend and mentor, and a leading scholar on the subject of leadership. He and I have devoted

8. David C. McClelland and David Burnham, "Power Is the Great Motivator," *Harvard Business Review*, Jan./Feb. 1995, 2–11.

9. James L. Fisher, *The Power of the Presidency and Presidential Leadership: Making A Difference* (New York: American Council of Education/Macmillan, 1984).

many hours to discussing the subject of power, and I owe him much for the thoughts that I am about to present. Fisher borrows, and I will too, from the paradigm created by sociologists French and Raven[10] to explain the sources of power and their consequences.

Coercive power. This is the least effective but, sadly, the most often used kind of power. It relies on threats and punishment to bring compliance. If the goal is to induce long-lasting change or commitment to you as a leader, it's not effective. People have many ways to subvert goals, such as sick leave abuse, carrying things home, loafing on the job, and tardiness. And they have many ways to get back—at you. Psychologists now use the term *passive-aggressive* to describe those who seem to be going along with you and agreeing with whatever you say but really haven't bought in. They are, in fact, finding clever ways to be noncooperative.

Coercive power can't be used often, but don't say you will never use it. Sometimes sanctions are necessary if you are an employer or if you have a teenager at home. It may be the last resort, but don't rule it out completely, particularly the *threat* of sanctions. I view myself as a humane, concerned person, but that hasn't kept me from occasionally firing people, knowing the effect fell not only on the individual but on many others who would be more apt to get with the program. That's one use of power—not the best one. Use it sparingly.

Reward power. Here we're giving rewards—intrinsic or extrinsic—to those whose behavior we like. As good parents know, rewarding good behavior is usually more effective than punishing bad behavior. But even this kind of power has limits. Fisher found no evidence that reward power alone could ensure long-lasting loyalty or commitment to an institutional cause. Part of the problem is that no reward can ever be enough, especially in today's knowledge-driven world, where, as you saw earlier, most of us believe we're in the top 5 percent in terms of intelligence and performance. There's a place for longevity awards, merit awards, raises, plaques, and all the accoutrements used to say to someone, "Job well done," and, implicitly, "I know you will continue." It's a good use of power but, alone, it's not enough and it won't last. Remember how we talked about sources of job satisfaction and dissatisfaction?

10. J. R. P. French and B. Raven, "The Two Faces of Power," *Journal of International Affairs* 24 (1969): 141–54.

Eliminating the dissatisfaction of employees doesn't necessarily make them satisfied in the long run.

Legitimate power. This is power given to an individual because of his position. I had a certain amount of power as chancellor or president of major universities. Office managers are ascribed a certain amount of power. Moms have power in the family. Wise leaders use this form of power as a platform for the structure and authority they need to lead.

It is very important that you, as a leader, behave the way people expect you to. That is, if you're in a church working group, wearing a tux to the meetings won't enhance your position. Wearing jeans to a formal gathering won't help either. You can and probably should be slightly better dressed than the others, but your legitimacy derives from behaving as expected, and people don't want you to be extreme in dress or appearance. I mentioned earlier an instance when a heavy snowstorm disabled an entire Midwestern state. The governor happened to be vacationing in Florida at the time and employed extraordinary measures to get back to her home state. Now, she could do nothing about the snow or its removal, but she had to be there—to be visible and to show that she cared. It was what the people expected of a legitimate leader. Legitimate power, then, is important, but you can lose it very quickly if you don't fit the role of leader.

Expert power. This is the most long-lasting type of power. Woody Allen once said "to be successful all you have to do is show up 80 percent of the time." I don't think Allen is entirely right—it takes more than that—but I can tell you that if you don't show up you can't lead. Leaders often are not given power because of their legitimate title; rather it flows from other means. Among them are: (1) a track record demonstrating expertise in such areas as computing, decision making, and group work; (2) personal qualities such as energy, intelligence, and interpersonal skill; (3) a sense of history; (4) the ability to resolve conflicts; (5) knowing the right people, being able to work with them, and getting things from them, and (6) being able to write well.

Expert power is something that every one of us can develop—we can find what we're best at. In the process, we will become the "go to" person in areas where we are better than others. In today's world, whoever fixes our software program has enormous power over us and makes a plethora of decisions for us.

Charismatic power. We use this power to gain affection, respect, and trust.

We create good feelings. Charismatic people light up the room and make people want to march. Charismatic leaders inspire others to follow. At the least, they are respected; at the most, they are revered.

While some charismatic power may be innate, much of it can be learned. Likewise, you can easily lose it by not acting like a leader. Or by attempting to be everyone's friend. Or by exposing all of your personal problems. Or by being a phony. Too often, charismatic leaders tend to be either revered or vastly unpopular. Martha Stewart, who has charismatic, legitimate, and expert power, is a good example. Many of her fans, mesmerized by her personality and her charisma, came to her support during her legal difficulties. Others seemed gleeful about her dilemma, not caring about what she did or didn't do and just happy to see a charismatic person fall. Charismatic leaders can fall very hard!

Here are some of the traits, characteristics, and behaviors of charismatic people: creating vision, enthusiasm, optimism, energy, persistence; remembering people's names (I flunk here); and making an impressive appearance. It helps to be charismatic.

Fisher maintains that over time even the most charismatic person sees his effectiveness lost as people begin to perceive him as really quite ordinary — just like them. This poses an important question: can charisma be acquired through effective leadership? I believe that much of it can. I've seen leaders grow on people to the point where their noncharismatic traits make them appear charismatic. They are in it for the long run and seem to get stronger every year. It is said that Abraham Lincoln was "charismatically challenged" in the conventional sense, and yet he was described as having "dogged tenacity," which, over time, created his charisma.

Perhaps you should see charisma as something to strive for — through your mannerisms, your behavior, your efforts to inspire, and your persistence in the face of difficulty. In other words, act like a leader!

Exercising Power

What good is having this information? It is good only if you understand it and are willing to work to increase your sources of power. The person given legitimate power must keep working to deserve it. Any one of us can develop power through the expertise that we have. Some of us are blessed with charisma, and we can find ways to use that quality, albeit carefully.

In most situations we use some of each source and a lot of others. For example, just a touch of coercive power, occasionally rebuking someone way out of line, providing recognition and other rewards, knowing what we're doing (expert power), and using the legitimate power given to us, can result in our getting a lot done. And if we're not given legitimate power, we still can offer rewards and currencies, develop expertise in something useful, and act and dress like a leader. Why not try it?

But how about relationships with those above us—they seem to have all the power. How can we use our personal power to make a difference?

First, it helps to know that it is possible for you to have power. We already discussed that. Second, you need to really understand your boss and her style of working. Kotter[11] believes that you need to know whether your boss is a good listener or a better reader and what decision-making style she prefers. Don't be unrealistic or cynical about your boss. No one, including your boss, has encyclopedic knowledge. Neither is your boss your evil enemy or your best friend. Figure out how to make yourself useful in your own way.

In summary, power is yours for the taking. Use it well and use it ethically. And don't confine yourself to one source.

Reality Exercise. Describe some of the leaders in your life—at work, in community service, at home—in terms of their power. Look specifically for those who seem to have greater power than their positions would dictate. What qualities led them to possess these powers?

Self-Awareness Exercise. Begin thinking about how you can be more powerful in areas that are most important to you at work or in your personal life. Which of the sources of power work best for you now? Which, with practice and greater understanding, can make you even more powerful? Develop and carry out a plan to make yourself more powerful.

11. Kotter, *Leading Change.*

Decision Making: An Art and a Science

> *Effective people do not make a great many decisions.*
> *They concentrate on the important ones.*
> —Peter Drucker, *The Essential Drucker*

> *In decision making, there is a two-part formula: Part*
> *one is use the formula P = 40 to 70 in which P stands*
> *for the probability of success and the numbers indicate*
> *the percentage of information acquired. Part two is that*
> *once information is in the 40 to 70 range, go with your*
> *gut.*
> —Colin Powell, *The Leadership Secrets*
> *of Colin Powell*

> *It's better to make a decision quickly and be right 7*
> *times out of 10 than to delay while searching for the*
> *perfect solution.*
> —Colin Powell, *The Leadership Secrets*
> *of Colin Powell*

> *When it's good enough, it's good enough.*
> —Buzz Shaw

Each of us makes numerous decisions in a day. Mostly, they're minor but sometimes they're life altering, such as considering a new job, a marriage, or a critical work-related project. Many scholars have studied decision making. Much of the scholarship is complex and helpful, if one wishes to make a career of learning everything about it. From my experience and from what I've read, I'll boil down this decision-making conundrum into nine points:

Remember the importance of vision, mission, and values. You will recall from an earlier chapter that effective leaders are the keepers of the vision, mission, and values. The best way to be a keeper is to use mission, vision, and values as a backdrop in making major, or even small, decisions. When Syracuse University restructured financially (over $60 million cut from its base budget),

the reductions were designed to reinforce our mission (to be *the* student-centered research university) and our values of quality, diversity, innovation, service, and caring. This meant that our cuts were strategic, not across the board. Our beliefs formed an important backdrop for those decisions.

Involve others. This doesn't mean that everyone gets to make a decision or that everyone's opinion is equally important. It does mean, however, that the more information you receive, at least to a point, the better able you'll be to weigh matters and, with a little luck, make a good decision. Before our restructuring program was announced, I asked over ten committees to suggest important policy principles that would help guide our decision making. Consultants also were brought in to offer their views, and the overall university community was encouraged, through forums, to give opinions. Before the plan was finalized, a rough draft was shared with university community members, giving them a chance to react, and hundreds did. This information and the specific policy recommendations from the ten-plus committees were taken into consideration before decisions were made. This method, of course, helped to obtain a buy in, but its biggest help was to guide me through tough decisions.

Use trade-off exercises. John Hammond et al.[12] describe at length the importance of using trade-offs in wise decision making. "Consider the debate that might go on in a town trying to decide whether public library hours should be cut to save money. The library advocate declares, 'preserving current library hours is much more important than cutting costs!' The fiscal watchdog says, 'No, we absolutely have to cut our budget deficit! Saving money is more important.' "

Hammond suggests that if the two sides focused on the actual amount of time and money in question—and looked at trade-offs—they might find it easier to reach an agreement. For example, if cutting two hours one morning a week saves $250,000 annually, the library advocate might agree that the harm to the library would be small compared to the amount saved, especially considering other possible uses for the money. If instead the savings were a mere $25,000 annually, even the fiscal watchdog might agree that the harm to the library wouldn't be worth the savings.

After Syracuse University's restructuring, we still faced major challenges (that never changes). To achieve our mission, we still needed to attend to a plethora of items. More about that later; for now, here's one illustration: we needed to improve our faculty and staff salary situation, so we developed a list of trade-offs showing various ways of meeting that and other objectives. Here is how it worked: suppose we wanted to raise salaries by 8 percent in one year. It could have been justified, but to do so, we would have needed to find some trade-offs. One would have been to reduce the size of faculty and staff, assuming that a smaller, more motivated group would be more productive. Or, we could have reduced the budget in other areas. Or, we could have imposed a tuition increase of roughly 10 percent.

The trade-off exercise was extremely helpful. Explained at a variety of forums, it helped members of the campus community understand that trade-offs would be necessary. It also helped get their opinions.

12. John Hammond, Ralph Geeney, and Howard Raiffa, "Even Swaps: A Rational Method for Making Trade-Offs," *Harvard Business Review*, Mar./Apr. 1998, 3–11.

In spite of the need, we ultimately did not grant an 8 percent salary increase because the consequences of doing that—reducing the size of faculty and staff, reducing operating budget lines, or raising tuition that high—simply were not practical.

Trade-off exercises can be used in far more sophisticated situations and also in those that don't involve a lot of detail. It's simply a way of thinking, and once you think that way, you can come up with the right exercise for the situation.

Please, make a decision. You saw from General Powell that you don't always have all the information you need. At some point, a decision has to be made. In this fast-paced world, particularly the business world, not making a decision often means ending up with a wrong decision by default. Drucker tells us that at some point we must go forward. Sometimes, no decision can be a very bad decision.

Be prepared to celebrate bad decisions. When you make them, analyze what went wrong, learn from it, and include it in your planning to avoid making the same mistake again. If someone you work with or who works for you made a mistake, the worst thing you can do is to criticize him, privately or publicly. If you're in the game, you're going to make a lot of decisions, some of them bad. Some organizations actually will celebrate a bad decision by bringing everyone together and talking about it, in effect praising whoever had the guts to make a decision, even if it turned out wrong.

In my early career, as an academic vice president I chaired the academic standards committee of an eastern public university. We were discussing how to be more flexible in our grading while maintaining high standards. I argued that if a student repeated a course and earned a better grade, she ought to get

"A decision is a judgment. It is a choice between alternatives. It's rarely a choice between right and wrong. It is at best a choice between 'almost right' and 'probably wrong.' But more often it is a choice between two courses of action, neither of which is probably more nearly right than the other."

—Peter Drucker, *The Essential Drucker*

"The eagle does not hunt flies." — Mike Royko

that grade instead of averaging it with the earlier grade. I believed that what a person knows at a given time was more important than the process by which they acquired that knowledge. One committee member cynically opined that if we're going to do that, why not just eliminate Fs?

This being the mid-1970s, a number of committee members took the idea seriously and enthusiastically said, "Why not?" The situation turned quickly. I was somewhat doubtful but supportive (my mistake). We developed a new grading system: A, B, C, D, no credit. Now you wouldn't be penalized for the worst grade that you could get; it wouldn't affect your average. What happened? Ds just about disappeared. Not only did students who were expecting Ds opt to tank the class (instead of trying to improve themselves), we had students sitting on Bs and Cs who decided to give up because they wanted a higher grade.

It was a disaster.

Rather than defending it, I publicly said it was a disaster and took much of the blame. We quickly changed it, and while we didn't celebrate our bad judgment, we moved on as colleagues and friends.

Beware of type II errors. In statistics, a type II error is when we accept a finding as being true when in fact it is not.

Suppose a study showed we could predict how students would do in college, at a 95 percent confidence level. We would jump at the chance of using that information because current prediction models are much less confident. We wouldn't worry a whole lot about the possibility (5 percent) that a type II error could occur. That would be wise decision making. But what if the issue is hauling radioactive material across the country, and there's a 95 percent chance that nothing bad will happen? We wouldn't be willing to take that chance, although we're 95 percent certain. We probably wouldn't take it if we were 99.5 percent certain. A type II error here would be catastrophic. The art form here is knowing when you are faced with a potentially disastrous type II error. Avoid it at all costs.

Don't sweat the small stuff. Don't allow yourself to be bogged down in decisions that don't need to be made. By empowering others to grow and learn, you also empower them to make many decisions that you don't need to make. The more the better. And the happier they will be as employees. Also, some decisions don't even need to be made. Either they are too small to make a difference, or the problem just goes away.

Jimmy Carter, a great humanitarian whom most historians considered to be at best an average president, tried to master too many of the details of governing. It is said he even decided the process for scheduling the White House tennis courts.

Remember, though, making decisions about decision making is an art form. If you allow unqualified people to make major decisions and they blow it, you are accountable, and that's not good. If it's a major decision and you decide none is required, that's not good either. You need to be in touch with yourself and the situation.

Learn to use your intuition (gut). Alden Hayashi[13] believes that the higher you rise in an organization, the more your gut instinct comes into play. "You process the best information available, infer from it, and use your intuition to make a decision," he says. Colin Powell said the same thing.

I have a problem with taking this idea too far. You are told to trust your gut, but I think a better way is to understand your gut and trust it when it is reliable. Over the years I've learned that my intuition in certain areas is, I believe, quite good, and in other areas, it's average to above average. Yet sometimes I'd be better off doing the opposite of what my gut tells me. This is true of my sense of direction. I've become lost three blocks from my Paris hotel. I've driven the wrong way for a half hour when I thought I was going north, only to find that I was going south. Having a map makes me 30 percent better; asking for directions adds another 20 percent, but I'm still usually hopelessly lost. In these situations, I've learned not to trust my gut, but to rely on the good directional sense of my wife or others to get where I need to go.

So, thinking I understand myself pretty well, I trust my gut in some areas but not in others. Hayashi says another reason not to put too much emphasis on "gut" decisions is our tendency to overestimate our ability in just about everything—such as driving, knowing when our jokes aren't funny, and de-

13. Alden M. Hayashi, "When to Trust Your Gut," *Harvard Business Review*, Feb. 2001, 6–11.

tecting when people are lying. He quotes studies conducted by Paul Ekman, professor of psychology at the University of California, San Francisco, who found that we're actually a lot less capable than we like to think we are. The main problem, Ekman says, is that many of us never really find out whether our judgments are accurate. So, if we don't know when we've made mistakes, we can't learn from them. And we blithely continue to make the same ones.

What does it all mean? It means that our intuition is important, but we need to be in touch with ourselves to best know when it's a help or a hindrance.

Constantly check on your own personal motives and needs. If you don't, they will drive decisions without your really knowing it, and they can be bad decisions. It's helpful to work on being self-aware, but don't trust yourself that much. Ask colleagues and friends whose advice you respect what they think about certain decisions you're considering before making them. And if you're inclined to be that open, ask them if they believe any personal motives or needs are driving you. You don't have to change your mind about the decision, but it doesn't hurt to better understand your own motives and needs.

I have asked Mr. William Davis, former CEO and chairman of Niagara Mohawk Power Corporation, to share his views on leadership. Bill managed and led thousands of NiMo employees through financial restructuring, improved operations, and a major take-over.

DECISION MAKING | William E. Davis

One of the management tenets that I tried hard to implement as CEO at Niagara Mohawk was that decisions should, in general, be made as close to the customer as possible. Early in my tenure, we focused on trying to create an empowered workforce with the tools necessary to deal with issues at the most appropriate level of the organization. To the extent we were at all successful, this meant that decisions that made it to my level were the ones that no one else in the organization felt in a position to make, or, alternatively, wanted to be accountable for making. They tended to be the ones that were most "politically" sensitive or policy oriented and also were the ones that generally had no clear-cut right or wrong answers. At the same time, they were generally important to the future of the company and involved strongly held and differing viewpoints among those most affected.

At this level, the decision making process must, above all else, be viewed as fair and open to input from all involved. It's far more important, in most instances, that those involved feel like they had a fair shot at affecting the outcome and understand why the decision was made, than that they feel like the one "right" or "perfect" decision was made. What's most important is the degree of "buy in" that occurs afterwards.

This should not be interpreted as an endorsement of decision making by consensus. Although consensus approaches may be applicable in some situations, they are not, in my view, appropriate in the business world. Businesses are not democratic organizations. Consensus approaches to decision making tend to be too time consuming for the pace of the business world and tend to yield mediocre compromises rather than well-informed and courageous decisions.

So, with that as a backdrop, here are my thoughts on decision making:

Insist on "Completed Staff Work." By this I mean make sure you have all of the information you need to make an informed decision. Give all major constituencies a chance to be heard. Seek their input, and make sure you have the facts that inform the decision as well as their views on the preferred decision. Included within the scope of completed staff work is a determination and analysis of possible outcomes (including no action) and the impact of each possible outcome on key internal and external constituencies.

Seek input from outside the organization. For those decisions that are likely to affect the organization's reputation or key external constituencies, make sure you're not relying completely on internal input.

Be decisive. By this I mean don't let the process linger to the point that the decision is no longer meaningful by the time you make it. This sounds so straightforward as to be obvious, but it is one of the most important skills of a decision maker. Everyone is familiar with organizations whose decision-making process can be described as "paralysis by analysis." Knowing when you have enough of the factual, analytical, and "persuasive" input necessary for the decision at hand is critically important.

Inform all who have had input to the process what the decision is and why it was made. Fully explaining the decision to those affected is absolutely critical to getting their buy in. This is the step most often neglected by decision makers and, I believe, is the most common reason why decision-making processes fail. In order for people to line up behind a decision, even one that doesn't go their way, they have to feel that they've had a fair opportunity to be heard, that their input was considered, and that they understand why the decision was made.

Recognize that no decision is a decision. If no decision is the right decision, treat it as such and communicate it just as you would any other decision, including an explanation.

Where possible, for action-related decisions, communicate with the decision the initial action plan for implementation. Include as much as you can about the responsibility for implementation, the action steps necessary, and the timetable. [WILLIAM E. DAVIS]

In sum, practical ways are available to improve your decision-making ability. If my suggestions and those of others are helpful, it is because you apply them and think about decisions after they're made. This leads to a few exercises that will round out this section.

Self-Awareness Exercises. 1. As you read over the nine suggestions, which do you believe best describes you? Which are strengths and which could be strengthened? Do you have any weaknesses that you'll have to work around (as I've learned regarding my being geographically challenged)?

2. Analyze a decision you recently made. Had you known these suggestions before making the decision, would you have done anything differently? If so, what would you have done? If not, I'm assuming that the situation turned out the way you wanted.

3. Think of a decision you need to make soon. Think about how you would incorporate into the decision-making process the suggestions that I've made. Once you've made the decision, evaluate how things turned out.

The Leader as a Communicator

> *Great leaders are almost always great simplifiers, who can cut through arguments, debate and doubt, to offer a solution everyone can understand.*
>
> —Michael Korda

Earlier we discussed "communicating the vision" as a key to effective leadership. Dear reader, I acknowledge that this isn't my strongest area. But I believe I'm better than average in writing and speaking and in small-group conversations. However, I'm far from being the highly skilled professional, so I've asked an expert to give his views on what leaders must know about communication skills. Dennis Byrne has made his living in communications as a newspaper reporter, editor, and columnist, a public relations director for a Fortune 500 conglomerate, and now as a public relations consultant and freelance writer. I'm also providing sidebar comments from other respected and successful communicators whose insights you will find helpful. But first, allow me to state some of my observations.

Communication is much more than getting the word out. It involves listening. If you can enhance your ability to listen, you can better understand the perspectives and issues from the other side. You also set up favorable conditions that invite others to listen to you. No one really wants to listen to a bad listener. Pierce[14] says we need to participate in "whole body" listening as a

> "If you really want to know something, phrase your questions differently than if you're selling the idea."
> —Chris Argyris, *Strategy, Change, and Defensive Routines*

means of saying to participants, "what you have to say matters." She offers some characteristics of good listening:

• Show that you are genuinely present as a listener (whole body listening). Look at the person speaking; don't be doing something else while she/he is speaking; let your entire face and body show that you are paying attention.

• Listen with curiosity, and allow the speaker to finish his story without interruption. Reply or ask questions based on your genuine curiosity, and summarize what you're hearing so he knows he's been heard (remember our discussion on conflict resolution).

• Verbally and nonverbally, make the speaker know that she has been heard and understood. You might paraphrase what she has said and ask if you have it right.

Good communicators are good persuaders. This means more than simply telling your story, even if you're doing it effectively. Jay Conger[15] gives us the *dos* and *don'ts* of an effective persuader. The most prevalent mistakes are:

• Attempting to make our case with an upfront, hard sell. Conger calls this the John Wayne approach.

• Resisting compromise. Too often we see compromise as surrender rather than as an essential part of getting to yes. For people to buy in, they need to know that you're flexible enough to respond to their concerns and to find better ways of doing things.

• Thinking that the secret of persuasion lies only in presenting great arguments. Equally important are such factors as credibility; the ability to create a proper, mutually beneficial, frame for discussion; and the ability to make your arguments come alive through vivid language.

14. Kim Pierce, *Public Dialogue Consortium, Basic Facilitator Training Manual*, 2001, 48.

15. Jay Conger, "The Necessary Art of Persuasion," *Harvard Business Review*, May/June 1998, 87.

"In all ways possible seek to be respected. Don't worry about being popular. Don't behave in ways that create fear. Be reasonable and truthful. Be persistent and determined, but always flexible."
—Eric Mower, chairman and CEO, Eric Mower Associates, Inc.

• Assuming that persuasion is a one-shot effort. Persuasion involves listening to people, testing a position, developing a new position that reflects input from others, testing that, and trying again. Says Conger, "if this sounds like a slow and difficult process, that's because it is. But the results are worth the effort."

So then, how to persuade? We are more persuasive if we are open-minded, not dogmatic. When we're seen by colleagues as eager to hear their views and willing to change in response to their needs and concerns, they are more prepared to hear us. Here are Conger's four essential steps:

• Establish credibility. Self-assessment is important because most persuaders believe that they have far greater credibility than they in fact have. Credibility comes from having good relationships with people and expertise worth hearing.

• Frame for common ground. Find things in common that help make persuasion work. The more you can appeal to common values and common goals, the more likely the message will be heard.

• Provide evidence. The most effective persuaders use language in a particular way, supplementing numerical data with examples, stories, metaphors, and analogies to make their positions come alive. Mary Kay Ash, the founder of Mary Kay Cosmetics, regularly draws on analogies and metaphors to drive her point home. Here's one dealing with doing the impossible. "You see, a bee shouldn't be able to fly: its body is too heavy for its wings. But the bumblebee doesn't know that and it flies very well." Mary Kay says she encourages women to fly, and they do.[16]

• Connect emotionally. Facts are important, and credibility is essential. But a strong and accurate sense of a group's emotional state is very important.

16. Conger, "Necessary Art of Persuasion," 17.

"The biggest communications mistake that 'leaders' can make is not telling the truth. Whether it is to the media, to employees, or to other 'publics,' not telling the truth is the absolute communications sin.

"Most important, it is a betrayal of the trust invested in a leader. But it's also self-defeating on a practical basis. The truth always comes out. When it does, the credibility of the leader will be severely compromised. Innocent people could be hurt. And the career of 'the leader' could be left in ruins.

"Whether it is a politician denying he has accepted favors, a corporate CEO pushing up the stock price by exaggerating profits, or a university employee inflating his résumé, the result always is the same. The truth eventually comes to the surface. Among those who learned the hard way is George O'Leary, who had to resign as Notre Dame University's head football coach because he faked his résumé. So too are some Enron executives, who are facing the heat for allegedly falsifying the company's earnings reports. John Rowland was forced to resign in a federal investigation of corruption in his office. They are far from alone.

"The truth may be painful. Or it may work against a short-term objective. But in the long run, all you have is your credibility. The beauty of telling the truth is that you don't have to remember what you said. All you have to remember is the truth."

— Joyce Hergenhan, retired vice president for
corporate relations, General Electric

As Conger says, "Sometimes it means coming on strong, with forceful points. Other times a whisper may be all that's required."

In short, Conger is saying persuasion is more than selling a point. It is being open-minded, open to trying new things — and negotiating.

Being heard means being perceived as credible. You believe what you say, and you practice it. This eventually gets back to your character, which we'll talk about later. People now talk about walking the talk — actually practicing what they preach. And to be credible, you must be truthful. Note the sidebar.

Don't underestimate the importance of reinforcement. Earlier, I talked about Syracuse University's five core values. They were illustrated in speeches, articles, and awards given to exemplars of those values—any way we could find to reinforce them. That doesn't mean saying the same thing each time, but rather emphasizing the same points in different ways. One of the ways that we repeated the themes was through our internal publications. Below are some headlines illustrating how our university communications office produced articles for internal publications, over a short time, dealing with our five values:

Quality:
> "Entrepreneurship Program Earns Top Tier Honors."
> "SU's Maxwell School Repeats as Number One in *US News* Rankings."
> "SU's Human Resources Wins Prestigious Award."

Caring:
> "Closing the Gap: SU Makes Strides in Retention."
> "Fair Wage Initiative Sets New Minimum Pay Level at Syracuse University."
> "SU Wins Donlon Spirit of Excellence Award for Work Life Policies."

Diversity:
> "SU Celebrates Support for Lesbian, Gay, Bisexual, Transgender Community."
> "Mural Project Invites SU Community to Celebrate Diversity."
> "Student CAPS Success Initiative Is Established."

Innovation:
> "New Learning Community to Encourage Creativity, Entrepreneurship, and Interdisciplinary Learning."
> "SU Students Pioneer College Crime Watch Program."
> "State of the Art Robot Launched to Monitor Waters of Otisco Lake."

Service:
> "SU and ESF Students Build a Place to Call Home."
> "SU Expands Year-End Clothing and Food Drive."
> "Syracuse University's Literacy Corps Remembers Victims of 9/11 Attacks with Book Donation."

"Don't allow the tongue to short-circuit the brain."
— Eric Mower, chairman and CEO, Eric Mower Associates, Inc.

None of these articles made a big issue of the value it was describing, yet it was an effective way to reinforce something needing to be said, many, many times. And now, let's hear from our communicator.

WRITE SHORT | Dennis Byrne

If I've learned one thing from being a writer for three decades, it's the value of being "short." Verbosity is the enemy of good communications.

Yet, too many people can't help themselves. Under some sort of spell, they spill out pages of unnecessary words. Sadly, the words are left unread or unheard because who wants to jump into *that* briar patch to find their meaning?

Of course, everyone says she knows the value of precise writing. That's because everyone has been on the receiving end of windy writing or speaking. Understanding "short" isn't difficult; practicing it is.

First, cleanse yourself of what they taught you in school—to write long. Teachers assigned writing assignments by length. Students learned to pad their compositions until they reached the magical one hundred words. Or to throw in meaningless and unnecessary words until they coughed up the assigned five pages.

Rare was the teacher who told you to write only what was necessary, and then stop. Too many of us had it drilled into us that spewing out mountains of words is proof of competence, knowledge, and intelligence. Being brief signals your incompetence, ignorance, and stupidity.

So taught, excessive length becomes a lifelong habit. Need to impress your boss? Hand him a thick report. Want to persuade an audience? Pummel your listeners with a long PowerPoint presentation. Need to communicate the importance of a project to your team? Call a long, gabby meeting, especially after lunch, and hand out hefty guidelines. Want to have your every word read? Churn out volumes of thoughts, proposals, action plans, goals, guidelines, research, and project descriptions. Then, like lawyers do, call them "briefs."

How many valuable ideas has civilization lost for all time because they have been buried in a morass of unnecessary words? A literate society awaits the day when our teachers and bosses buy into the revolutionary idea that a piece of writing should be only "long enough" to cover the subject matter. If all it takes is a paragraph to do the job, then so be it; the writer has mastered the topic and conveyed his understanding with precision. Without wasting anyone's time.

When I was a columnist and editorial board member at the *Chicago Sun-Times*, the papers's most graceful writer, Bill Braden, undertook to produce a manual to help editors and reporters produce the best writing possible. After receiving thoughts on style, grammar, usage, and so forth from several coworkers, he arrived at my desk. I thought for a minute, tapped out two words, and handed them to him: "Write short." Bill understood, and left happy.

A friend and a legendary investigative reporter, upon his induction into the Chicago Journalism Hall of Fame, rambled on and on in his acceptance speech. Fred had a reputation for writing long, which burdened his editors, who had to cut deeply into his prose to fit the space. As he approached twenty minutes, I whispered to the city editor, to his stifled amusement, "He talks as long as he writes." Fred did so much to blur his own message that he communicated nothing. Although I respect him immensely, to this day I can't remember a thing he said.

The point is: unlike professional writers, who are disciplined by their editors, leaders rarely have anyone strong enough to tell them to make their messages short, precise, and clear. So, you'll have to do it, maybe the way I learned.

As a newspaper columnist, I was assigned a word count of about 750 words. Invariably, my first draft was too long. So, back I went, cutting out adjectives and adverbs. "Once again" became "again." Still too long, and back I went. Entire phrases and sentences vanished. Some I thought were jewels, too sweet, powerful, insightful, or informative to be crushed by the delete button.

Crushed they were. Because they were side streets, taking the reader away from the main highway. I began to understand that if the point of the column was important enough to be a column, then it didn't deserve to be diluted by digressions. The reader deserved better than to be forced to navigate back roads to find the point.

But as I shoehorned the copy into the allotted space, I noticed something.

The column got better. Leaner, stronger, more fluid, more pointed. Losing the fat sharpened and strengthened what remained. Spare writing is not barren writing. Precise writing is not necessarily colorless and boring.

If the secret to good communications is being short, then the secret to being short is knowing your point. Can you speak or write it in a sentence? Before you put one word on paper, can you tell *yourself* what you want to say? What's the one thought you want your readers or listeners to leave with? If you have no such point, then ask yourself: Why bother with this communication? Why burden your subordinates with another message from on high?

Notice what I'm saying: the actual writing is secondary to the planning, thinking, and logic that form the substance of your communication. When a writer sits before a blank page complaining that inspiration hasn't struck, he ought to ask himself: Do I know what I want to say? Once you do, the writing part comes easier.

No, I am not dismissing the importance of the style, eloquence, or delivery of a communication. Or the difficulty of writing. So here is the best source I know of to help you with the mechanics of writing: *The Elements of Style*, by Strunk and White. It's been around almost fifty years, but it still is the most effective, fundamental guide to writing in the business. In addition to the dry stuff (correct use of commas and apostrophes), it's also packed with great common-sense advice: use the active voice, place the emphatic word at the end of a sentence, do not explain too much, and write in a way that comes naturally. The book's inexpensive and, best of all, it's short.

Whether or not you master these skills (and who has the time?), you, as the leader, must set the tone for proper communication within your company, institution, office, or organization. You cannot allow ten-page executive summaries to preface thirty-page documents. Send it back with two options: get rid of the executive summary and tighten up the thirty pages—or get rid of the thirty pages and tighten up the executive summary. After all, if the writer appeared in your office in person, instead of on paper, how much of your time would you give him to elaborate, repeat, and stammer? Not much. Then why can't you demand better of something you're given in writing?

Lead by example; don't be afraid if a speech or presentation seems too short. I've never heard anyone complain about such a thing. More likely, you'll get prolonged applause and glowing reviews.

Don't be afraid of being conversational or chatty; be very afraid of using jargon because you think it makes you look smart. It only makes you look pompous.

You'll notice that in this essay I have violated some time-honored "rules." I don't shun sentence fragments because someone said they must not be used. I use fragments liberally. And I start sentences with conjunctions. I even found a place to use a dangling participle. I'm not for throwing the rules of grammar out the window, but they shouldn't be a straitjacket when they hinder good communications.

Don't feel that you have enough discipline to pull it off? Then appoint someone you trust to tell you when you're becoming a windbag. Someone who already knows the meaning of terse.

Of course, the receivers of communications have a burden to get and process the message. But as a leader, you ultimately have a burden as the initiator of the communication to see that it gets to everyone. You, the leader, have an obligation to be succinct and clear in communicating the meaning, to determine that the meaning was understood, and that action, if required, is taken. By definition, you cannot lead if you cannot communicate.

Communications Exercise. As originally submitted, my essay was almost 3,600 words. Too long; I cut it by about half. Then I cut more. And again. Still more can go, but I'll leave it to you. Go back and see how much more you can eliminate. [DENNIS BYRNE]

Reality Exercises. 1. Identify a business, government, education, or sports leader whom you perceive to be a top communicator. Explain the basis for your judgment.

2. Identify a well-known leader in one of these categories who is not, in your opinion, a good communicator. Explain what other qualities might help this person be a better communicator.

Self-Awareness Exercise. What about you? Having read my thoughts, those of Dennis Byrne, and other experts, how do you evaluate your communications understandings and skills? What areas do you need to work on? What specific plans might you put into operation to improve in those areas?

Leading in Times of Crisis

Sooner or later, every institution or organization faces a bona fide crisis, something of such enormity that to get ready for it is almost impossible. No matter how well an organization thinks it has prepared, the crisis quickly reveals gaping holes in its planning.

Crises are times that test all leaders, of all kinds—formal and informal—on all levels. September 11, 2001, was just such a time, at Syracuse University and elsewhere. Several years before that day, our campus had sustained a major storm that left power out, thousands of trees down, and extensive damage to some student housing complexes. Fortunately, no one was seriously injured. The entire campus was mobilized; the effort was outstanding, and very quickly we were back on our feet, although it took months to repair the residence buildings, and to plant trees.

We learned several things from that disaster:

1. All leaders, particularly the chancellor, must be extremely visible. Rapid and frequent communications are required.

2. Our faculty, staff, and students responded heroically. Highly capable, dedicated, and resilient people were ready to do whatever was necessary. Acts of personal heroism and kindness were numerous.

3. We knew that our planning mechanisms for crises were inadequate. The experience left us with an understanding, we thought, of what more we needed to do. Naturally, we began doing those things.

So, we survived that crisis, proud of our efforts to strengthen our planning.

Then came September 11th.

Our country and the university were forever changed. Our university community was particularly affected because thousands of our students and more than 100,000 of our alums come from the New York City and Washington, D.C., areas. While we were better prepared for a crisis this time, no organization could be completely ready for *this* disaster. So, in spite of our good planning, much of our efforts had to be ad hoc.

What follows is a chronicle of our activities from September 11 through October, and our observations about how to be better prepared next time. The precise way we went about things might not have been your way, but it gives you some idea of what needed to be done.

Syracuse University, Chronicle of Events, September 11, 2001

- An emergency Chancellor's Cabinet meeting was called for 11 A.M. Before this meeting, the university's Crisis Management Team assembled and began formulating plans to guide the remainder of the day—and the days ahead. The typical team of twelve key members grew to seventy people by midday.

- An information center was established in the office of the Vice President for Student Affairs, as well as centers in Hendricks Chapel and the Panasci Lounge. The centers ensured student access to information, services, and support as and when needed.

- Phone banks were made available in the Schine Student Center and the Women's Building so students could get in touch with their families.

- We agreed to gather as a university community at 3 P.M. in Hendricks Chapel. Several thousand students, faculty, and staff crowded in for the proceedings.

- A communications plan unfolded that consisted of twice-daily electronic briefings by e-mail and 3 P.M. briefings in the Chapel.

- Classes continued, except for the 3 to 4 P.M. period. Students who needed to attend to attack-related business were excused from class.

- Key student buildings, including the Schine Student Center and Hendricks Chapel, were open around-the-clock.

- Counselors and volunteer staff, trained in critical incident response during the summer of 2001, geared up for hall meetings and to provide student support as needed. More than 2,100 students participated in formal discussions in their residence halls.

- Many events were canceled or rescheduled out of respect for the tragedy and victims.

- Student needs were assessed quickly. For any student who lost a supporting parent, custodian, or spouse in the disaster, special financial aid consideration was given by the Office of Financial Aid. Full tuition would be provided to these students while they remained at Syracuse University. Further, students whose supporting parent, guardian, or spouse temporarily lost employment and/or income because of the attack became eligible for special grant assistance for the remainder of the academic year.

- An emergency response committee assisted faculty, staff, and students called to service.
- Students needing academic assistance because they were coping with the tragedy were referred to the Division of Student Support and Retention.
- Many on-campus ceremonies and vigils were held to honor the victims and to provide support to the campus community. Additionally, fund-raising events were sponsored to raise monies for victims' families and relief efforts.
- Alumni worldwide visited the SU website for news. The site received over 330,000 hits between September 11 and the end of the fall semester.
- Hundreds of students, faculty, and staff signed the Student Association's Sheets of Expression on the quad. Thousands more were moved by the thoughts recorded there. Opportunities for expression also were provided on the SU News Web site and reproduced in the *Syracuse Record*.
- Recreational activities were scheduled for students to ensure they keep a balance in their lives at a difficult time.
- Six working committees were established after September 11. One committee worked to prepare SU for challenges requiring swift and effective responses relating to transportation, inventory needs, access to buildings, and radio communications. Another committee developed a series of campuswide education forums related to the attacks and our country's response. A third committee worked to understand and address any special needs of students studying abroad through SU's Division of International Programs Abroad (DIPA). Other committees addressed emergency communications, campus safety issues, and call-to-service issues.
- A parking lot was closed to provide a landing site for helicopters bringing victims from New York City to University Hill hospitals for treatment.
- The SU community collected shirts and socks to serve the rescue workers in New York City. A seventeen-foot truck was needed to ship all the shirts and socks downstate.
- In the days following September 11th, a community in action came together on campus. The lines were very long for the Red Cross blood drive, and many students were turned away. Over two hundred pints of blood were collected. Hundreds more were collected from a later drive in Syracuse.
- DIPA programs kept in close communication with the university to explain precautions being taken and results of events. Standing policies and pro-

cedures were addressed. During Parents Weekend, a Study Abroad Fair was held, with a special breakout session on safety. Parents were reassured about the security steps taken and the overall approach to safety matters.

• Auxiliary Services sent supplies to the High School for Leadership in New York City, whose building was three blocks from the World Trade Center. New York City alumni mentored and provided stability to the shocked and anxious students.

• White ribbons were distributed to the community in support of the terrorism victims.

• Communications were made regarding safe mail handling, including mailings, e-mail, and Campus Safety Alerts.

• I sent a letter to all SU parents on October 9 to assure them of the precautions and steps SU took to ensure student safety and well-being.

These and other activities (to chronicle all that was done by each area would more than fill a book) were designed to help people who had particular needs. We lost more than thirty alums and an untold number of parents, relatives, and friends of our students and alumni, and we needed to provide healthy outlets for those who needed to express their anger, anxiety, and, in some cases, depression. Also, we needed an outlet for the thousands who wished to help others during this time (a healthy activity), and finally a means for members of the university community to discuss the significant policy and moral issues of September 11th.

We learned much.

What we learned was compiled and reported to me and to members of my cabinet. The most significant of the recommendations included creating a university-wide written crisis management plan and a protocol for response, including delineating ownership of each activity. We also learned we needed to train our staff members on the existence, content, and implementation of this plan.

Also, we needed to improve our communications, particularly with our off-campus students. Finally, we learned that while we had made great strides in our logistical planning, we needed to do much more. We formed a logistics committee, which was to develop procedures for emergencies. That group developed procedures dealing with preparation, response, and recovery. Those procedures are now in use.

We keep learning. We keep trying to improve our planning. Still, we know that none of these plans is complete. At the end of the day, the presence of capable, committed, resilient people who are willing to step up is by far our most important asset.

Personal Observations and Advice

If you are in a top leadership position, a major crisis likely will strike on your watch.

1. You must be everywhere. You must communicate often, stay cool and calm, and generously offer your praise, support, and compassion. It all rubs off on those looking to their leader(s) for guidance.

Here is a message that I sent to our alumni, in which I tried to incorporate my own advice:

A Message from the Chancellor

September 11, 2001, forever changed the country, the world, and your University. The gaping holes left in the ground in New York City and Pennsylvania and the gash in the side of the Pentagon were horrific symbols of a new world in which safety can never be taken for granted and in which the quest for peace must be redoubled.

The grief we at Syracuse feel over the unprecedented carnage is sharpened by the knowledge that thirty of our alumni are gone. Still others lost family members, colleagues, and friends.

You have reason to be very proud of your University in this time of crisis. Reaction to the September 11 events was immediate and effective. A crisis team of administrators, faculty, and staff gathered within hours of the attacks. Their efforts culminated that first day in a University gathering at 3 P.M. in Hendricks Chapel.

I watched in amazement and gratitude as some two thousand students streamed in. They filled every seat, even those traditionally reserved for the choir, and they lined the walls on both floors.

They heard words of comfort from chaplains, the vice chancellor, and me, and they were encouraged to support each other and to talk freely about the incidents and their meanings.

Counselors were dispatched to every corner of the campus. Buildings remained open well past normal hours. Food and beverages were available around the clock.

And the community gathered in grief and in resolve to learn the truth.

A blood drive the next day saw members of the University line up by the thousands, far too many to accommodate at that point. A call for clean shirts and socks for the New York City rescue workers resulted in hundreds of pounds of clothing being collected on campus and sent to New York by tractor-trailer.

The work goes on, and so does our renewed sense of purpose as a university. As the nation and the world struggle to find answers, we know we must be true to the essence of a university—a place where the search for truth can go on unhindered by fear of reprisal. This is a unique role we have been granted, one we must carry out if we are to have a present worth preserving and a future worth our hope.

Sincerely,

Kenneth Shaw

Chancellor

2. If any turf problems spring up in response to the emergency (we had none), they must be resolved immediately with everyone reminded of the higher purpose of the work.

3. Smother people with praise—those doing the superhuman, those helping the emotionally traumatized, and those trying to be brave.

4. After it's all over, you must question how you can improve upon the processes. Not immediately, as people need time to grieve and to be sufficiently proud of their extraordinary efforts. But surely later.

5. Even though I've said that you need to be everywhere, you also must take care of yourself—getting as much sleep as you can, eating the right foods, and exercising, where and when you can. This is not a time for you to have a physical or emotional breakdown. It's time to rise above the problems, so you need to take care of yourself.

Doing all the right things still produces only two guarantees: one, there will be another crisis, with luck on someone else's watch; and two, in spite of all of the planning, ad hoc arrangements still will be necessary. Most fundamentally, you still will end up relying on the capable, committed, resilient people who make your organization run.

Reality Exercise. You are the principal of a medium-size elementary school in a sedate suburban community. Last evening, a tornado came through town and tore off your school's roof. You're told about this at midnight. Think through what you would do to deal with this crisis, write the steps you would take, and prioritize them.

5

Leading Groups

How often have you heard these words?

"Our management group will meet tomorrow."

"You will chair our task force on cost savings."

"I'm nominating you for the United Way Committee."

"We need some new ideas. Let's get some people together and be creative."

"This is a decision that must be right—and our employees must buy into it. That will be your group's job."

Do you regard them with dread, or as a challenge? As a pain, or as a way to achieve a worthy goal?

Obviously, the activities all involve groups. That means: another meeting. We are told that executives spend about a third of their time in some kind of group or meeting. But you don't have to be an executive to have your life affected by group activity. Most organizations, large or small, utilize work teams. You can't escape. So why not learn how to guide groups toward productive outcomes?

This chapter is longer than most for a reason: the importance of group work in our lives today. Unfortunately, for all the time that we spend in groups, the skills needed for making that time productive get disproportionately less attention in leadership and management courses. People who actually engage in business are more likely to place a much higher value on communication, cooperation, and teamwork than those of us who write about and teach leadership. I tell college students that they will go far if they can communicate well, know how to deal with conflict, and can be an effective member of a team.

Groups Can Be Good or Bad

Groups can be destructive, ineffective, conservative (nothing ever done for the first time), and uncreative, if handled poorly—and they usually are. Consider these observations made by disgruntled group participants:

"A committee is a group of the unfit, appointed by the unwilling, to do the unnecessary."

A committee is "a group of individuals who can do nothing that collectively meets to decide that nothing can be done."

"The trouble with committees is that things are discussed but rarely decided, and if they are decided, they don't get executed."

"A camel is a horse designed by a committee."

Despite such sentiments, I've found that groups *can* be efficient, effective, courageous, creative, and useful in legitimatizing necessary decisions. Whether groups are productive or destructive depends on us.

So, in this chapter you will learn: (1) the most important things to understand about groups; (2) the constructive use of group roles; (3)how to recognize and deal with destructive group roles; (4) how to run a meeting; and (5) how to stimulate group creativity.

You won't become an expert in this short time, but you can learn enough from this information and your assignments to grow on your own.

The Importance of Knowing Group Purpose, Size, and Function

Here is what you first need to understand about groups.

Group purpose. Know it and be able to explain it—or decide not to bother meeting. Groups cannot be effective if they don't know what they are supposed to do.

Group size. It tells you what approach to use. We ignore the question of group size at our peril.

Group function. Task and/or socioemotional? Both functions are important in any group; neither can be ignored. But understanding the differences between the two functions is quite important.

Group Purpose

People will remain members if they know a group has a purpose, if they have an incentive to be involved, if the goals are difficult (but not impossible), and if the group's activities are appropriate for the purpose.

It is a waste of everyone's time to meet without a clear purpose. It is the biggest mistake made in meetings. To quote a soldier's lament in an old semi-humorous song about Custer's Last Stand: "What am I doing here?" If people are thinking or asking that question, the group is in trouble; nothing will get done. Know the purpose of the group, and then be able to explain its purposes in general terms, and if the group meets often, in specific terms (goals).

What are some purposes of groups?

To give information. People gather to hear something. This is not an uncommon group purpose. The CEO wants her top people to know exactly how she feels on an issue, to communicate news from the home office, and so forth.

Information is given, questions are asked and answered, and people get on with their business. Little discussion occurs, and little is encouraged. Information meetings serve a legitimate purpose, yet, and unfortunately, they are held more than needed and expected. Or the convener, droning on, strays from the topic. This type of meeting can become a place to doodle, daydream, and learn to sleep with your eyes open. Or it can be a quick, efficient way to dispense information.

To give and receive information. The convener is interested in more than giving information; he also wants participants to share with everyone else important and relevant information they possess. Here, lines of communication are kept open.

This kind of meeting is very important because keeping everybody informed helps to promote a common purpose. It often leads to, "Now, let's talk about how we can work together to achieve our mutual and separate goals." Meetings that are held to give and receive information need not be long. If they are, time is wasted.

In today's high-tech world, you can exchange information in both kinds of groups via the Internet, telephone, or videoconferences. Still, face-to-face is often the best way to give and receive information.

To make decisions or to advise a decision maker. Alas, many well-intended meetings never get to this point. Information is given and shared, but it stops there and everyone goes home.

When decisions need to be made, groups must be appropriately structured. This requires planning, leadership, and group skills that you will learn. Getting bogged down after information is given and received, as most groups do, is not the fault of involving more than one person in decision making. It is a question of group leadership and followership. Effective groups can make decisions, and they can give good, sound advice. But they must be led.

To develop new ideas. Here new approaches are expected, and the creative process unfolds. "We must leapfrog the competition with new ways of doing things to survive." For some, solitary activity works best. For others, a small brainstorming group allows members to learn other insights, piggyback on them, and arrive at new approaches. Again, groups often fail to fashion new ideas not because groups inhibit the creative process, but because most participants don't know how to use groups productively.

To resolve differences. When conflicts occur, a group often is gathered to resolve it. But differences aren't resolved if the group leader has no skills for conflict resolution — something you've already learned.

To achieve understanding and acceptance of a decision. When decisions must be made, followers must understand the decision and the reasons for it. Here the leader is less interested in getting viewpoints than in selling an idea. She must "rally the troops." Too often these meetings end up with the leader selling and no one buying. Even an accomplished speaker can lose the group in this type of meeting. But sometimes this approach must be used.

So understanding and explaining a group's purpose is essential. Know that these six possible purposes are not discrete entities; meetings or groups may have more than one purpose. For a group to be effective, you must know its purpose (or purposes) while working for quality and legitimate decisions. Quality decisions are those that are good for the situation at hand; legitimate decisions are those that the group will accept and be willing to support in their implementation. By effectively using group purpose you are more apt to achieve good, legitimate decisions.

> *Reality Exercise.* Think of a work or social group to which you belong that meets regularly. Describe the purpose of the meeting. Do members know its purpose? Does it stick to its purpose? Does knowledge and acceptance of the purpose seem to matter? If this group is having "purpose problems," what could be done to make it more effective?

Group Size

Size dictates the approach you will use in managing groups. Failure to understand this reality is a huge mistake. Consider these typical hurried judgments about group size:

"We've got a problem — let's get twenty or thirty of our best people together — hash it out and come up with a solution."

"We'll bring in our top fifty people from around the nation and meet — we'll work out our differences and reach consensus. We won't leave until it's done."

"The group is too large for us to get any kind of opinions—we'll have to wing it."

That's not the way to do it. Group size (along with the group's purpose) determines how we structure our meetings and the techniques we use in them.

Let's start with the *principle of least group size*. A group must be large enough to include individuals with all the relevant skills for problem solving, but no larger. Having too many people—our biggest mistake—turns the meeting into an Easter egg hunt, with some participating and most watching. I acknowledge that a few participants might be added for legitimacy purposes, but make it as small as you can. Below is an explanation of a number of group sizes, along with the advantages and disadvantages of each.

Small groups of two or four. Usually this fails to include a wide enough range of abilities to generate a sufficient variety of views. This size is okay for a few activities, but it generally crimps the generation of the widest range of views and makes the less participative feel threatened. In a slightly larger group, the reticent can participate less but still feel accepted and effective.

Groups of three. This size meeting often result in two people dominating the discussion and the agenda. The third person often keeps quiet and goes along. Of course, the third person becomes important if the other two can't agree. He then becomes the center of attention.

Groups of five to eleven. This size is optimal. With groups this size, we can obtain a variety of views and avoid the "obligation to talk" felt by some in a smaller group. Shoot for a group size of five to eleven people if you want participation, satisfaction, agreement, and a good decision.

Larger groups—more than eleven. As groups become larger, methods must change. When they don't, you've got problems. In a badly run larger group, the most talkative members take most of the time, the majority of people talk much less, the somewhat shy never talk, and all are dissatisfied with their involvement. In the end, a few constant talkers may dominate the outcome.

But know that there are good reasons why larger groups can be formed—for the skills needed, and often to make the decision legitimate. Larger size is not a problem if techniques change. The larger the group, the more the convener must dictate the process. If that doesn't occur, the group will not function well. Even with groups of a thousand, we can find techniques that work. Later in this chapter, we'll talk about what can be done to make groups of all sizes effective.

Group Function: Task and/or Socioemotional

While most groups involve task and socioemotional functions, in most cases we want more task.

For our purposes, task refers to getting a particular job done—improving productivity, accuracy, quality, or speed, or assigning people to work in a volunteer effort. In other words, accomplishing the instrumental purposes of the group. Socioemotional function refers to personal needs and group needs, which are connected with relationships. Those needs involve the feelings group members have toward one another, and they affect the group's cohesiveness and morale.

To a certain extent, satisfaction with the group's interaction and its work depend on meeting socioemotional needs. All of us need to affiliate, to feel that we belong. And much of our time in groups is spent this way. In its extreme, very little else gets done. Examples are the coffee klatch that extends into lunch, or major decisions being held in abeyance while golf games are discussed or birthdays celebrated.

But socioemotional functions are very important. We need to feel good about the group and our role in it. Some groups are almost totally socioemotional—ten minutes for task, the rest for fun. Nothing is wrong with that, if it's the group's true purpose. Many service clubs and church groups focus on expressions of friendship and having a good time. The important point is that all groups, even those that are extremely task-oriented, also must have a socioemotional function.

Effective groups seem to be a combination of both task and socioemotional functions. (Actually, few groups exist in either pure form.) It is important to know that the average group spends about 50 percent of its time meeting socioemotional needs; you can't expect 100 percent task. If you do, you'll lose your membership. Even if they still come, they won't be involved because the task has become too heavy.

I try to shoot for 70–80 percent task in working groups, thus allowing for socioemotional needs to be met while not allowing them to get out of hand.

For the task-driven: honoring birthdays and anniversaries, or expressing collective concern about a colleague's problem, such as a child's illness or parent's death, are some ways to meet socioemotional needs. As the work gets tougher, emphasizing the socioemotional aspect is all the more important.

If you can get to 70 percent task, be happy. You can try to push further, but watch to see if the group is getting stressed. You might be pushing too hard.

What good is knowing this? It helps us decide how to make the group more productive. For example, a group leader seeing a meeting straying from its purpose might say, "We spend 75 percent of our time talking and patting one another on the back. We need to get down to work." If the group is getting weary, she might say, "We've been at it all day; let's take a break," or "Several of us suggested we knock off early today and have a drink together. We worked very hard today. What do you think?"

> *Reality Exercise.* Analyze one of your own groups. Does it seem to be working? How could it be more task-oriented? How could it be more socioemotional? What do you believe would be the optimal task/socioemotional ratio for this group?

Effective Decision Making for Medium-Sized and Large Groups

Given what we've said about the advantages of small groups, you might wonder why there should ever be a medium-sized or large group. If the goal is to keep the group as small as possible, why go large?

Remember our earlier lesson: group decisions must be sound and legitimate. Often, arriving at a good solution isn't enough; lending strong support (legitimacy) to a good solution also is necessary. Also, sometimes—but not often—a large group is required to include all the needed expertise.

Two Approaches with Limited Utility: Majority Rule and
100 Percent Agreement

Majority rule. This is a less desirable approach to medium- and large-group decision making. Legislators, for example, typically follow the "majority rules" principle: discussion, maybe much acrimony, and finally a vote. The majority wins. Sometimes there's no other choice. However, if the vote is close, a sizeable number of supporters have been lost. Something that is supported by 55 percent and strongly opposed by 45 percent runs the risk of never being properly implemented. While sometimes unavoidable, winning by a bare majority can cause real buy-in problems.

One hundred percent agreement. Then should we shoot for 100 percent agreement? This is the Quaker approach to decision making—keep at it until everyone agrees. When someone disagrees, ask him what's needed for him to come on board. Then ask the others if they are willing to change. Keep plugging away until you have secured unanimous agreement.

Obviously, this makes the group very cohesive. Obviously, too, coming to a decision becomes very difficult. The approach works when the group, like Quaker society, is closely knit, and social control can be imposed on dissenters.

The advantage of majority rule is the ability to reach quick decisions. The advantage of 100 percent agreement is that those decisions are the most legitimate and binding (if we live long enough).

There are better ways. Here are some approaches that can work for you when dealing with medium-sized and large groups.

The consensus-seeking approach. Its essential principles are:

1. Plan. Because the group is large, the purpose should be clear. Materials should be sent out in advance, and the meeting's precise goals should be stated.

2. At the meeting, state the problem as carefully and specifically as possible. For example: "We are given 5 percent increases for raises. Our job is to determine a structure for giving out this money." Or "We have a major financial crisis; our bottom line expenses must be reduced by 5 percent. It is our job to recommend how." Or "Management is willing to increase our fringe benefits package by 10 percent. It is our job to recommend how these dollars be spent."

3. Ask for suggestions or solutions. Don't judge the ideas; simply keep track of them.

4. Once all the ideas are listed, consider each alternative. Ask supporters of each approach to indicate their reasons. Then ask opponents for theirs. The

group leader *must* manage the process! Once a particular reason has been given, either negative or positive, don't allow it to be repeated. If people can't contain themselves, allow them to say "ditto." This prevents hearing the same thing over and over (not necessarily dysfunctional in a small group but deadly in a large one).

5. Once alternatives are presented and pros and cons outlined, press for a straw vote. How many favor option 1? option 2? option 3? option 4?

6. After the straw vote on that issue, continue the discussion in the following fashion:

    a) If there is a clear consensus (65–80 percent), you may want to declare huge support and see if those with contrary votes will go along. Or just declare victory and move on.

    b) If the straw vote was close, more time is needed.

        (1) Ask opponents to indicate what modifications they'd like to see to make the option more acceptable.

        (2) Engage in the same discussion as before, where the pros and cons of suggested modifications are outlined.

        (3) Then, as before, take straw votes on the several refinements.

        (4) If a clear preference emerges, you're home free. Move on.

        (5) If there still is no clear preference, choose to repeat the process or move on.

        (6) Move on to the next issue, using the same approach.

7. Once all the issues are resolved, summarize the agreements.

8. After the summary, ask for a straw vote on the entire package.

Assuming at least two-thirds agree to the package, you might want to appoint a small group to flesh out the details for a final vote. Or you might just want to declare victory and move on.

Sometimes, after all this discussion, a strong consensus still will not be reached. But you haven't wasted everyone's time; all participants have had a chance to present their views, refine major issues, and vote on separate options and the total package.

This approach doesn't guarantee total agreement. It does provide for involvement in a controlled way. Without that control, attempting to reach agreement with large groups is nearly impossible, unless its members agree beforehand. If so, don't have the meeting!

The Nominal Group Technique

The nominal group is designed to get member input, while restricting communication among its members.

Why would you ever want to limit member communication? Perhaps because the group is too large or because the issues are so emotional nothing would get done. The nominal group technique depersonalizes things by defending against the dominant or overly talkative members while giving everyone a chance to participate. It is simple and, at times, effective.

Nominal groups don't actually need to meet, or if they do, the interaction is minimal. Here is how it works:

1. Silent generation of ideas. After the leader presents the issue, participants, including the leader, silently write a list of alternative courses of action. This should take about five minutes. No conferring; only silent attention occurs. For example: "What kind of compensation system should we establish for the 5 percent pay increase that management is handing out?" Alternatives presented: (1) a total merit system; (2) a combination of merit and across-the-board increases; (3) all increases across-the-board.

2. Listing ideas. After ideas about alternative actions have been handed in, the leader writes down the proposals where all can see them, and calls for any additional ideas to add to the list. This is done briefly. Now all ideas are there for people to see.

3. Brief discussion of the suggestions. This is for clarification, not evaluation, to be sure that all suggestions are understood.

4. Preliminary vote. Ask everyone to vote privately. They could weight good ideas as four or five, bad ideas as one, and middling ideas as two or three. From this analysis, determine which approaches are kicked out and which remain. If you have started with only a few ideas, you may want to leave some of the middle ones in. If one approach has a strong consensus, you probably have a winner.

5. Discuss the preliminary vote. This tactic helps ensure that everyone understands the apparent group preferences and allows for clarification. Also, a brief opportunity can be provided to discuss pros and cons of the most popular ideas.

6. Final vote. Participants now privately rank their most desirable options

from the list generated by the preliminary vote. The option with the best over-all ranking wins.

In a relatively short time, you have moved a medium-sized or large group to a decision. You can be sure that at least a majority of members agree with a common approach. Also, everyone knows he or she has been involved and that his or her ideas have been received and considered.

The disadvantages of this approach are obvious: it lacks spontaneity and overlooks some potential hitchhiking of ideas.

However, for a large group, you have arrived at a legitimate and sound decision. At least the group will think so.

Let's deal with the "but what ifs." What if, after the vote:

1. The idea needs much more fleshing out? Then you can turn to a smaller group of five to eleven participants. The larger group's work is done; allow it to go home. Keep its members informed but not involved.

2. Only a bare majority supports a given view? You might then break into smaller groups using the consensus-seeking approach to see if you can get wider support. Or you might simply go with what you have.

3. What if the group is too large for the available room? Nothing prevents you from breaking the larger group into smaller groups and using a number of rooms. Or you could handle the issue by mail or over the Web.

The Delphi Approach

The Delphi approach is really the mail version of the nominal group. Using e-mail, it can be very quick and effective and useful for very large or even small groups. (Although with small groups it is probably better to just get together.) The procedures are simple. A series of assignments are prepared and analyzed by a "gatekeeper," with each assignment based on responses to the previous one. Here is how it works.

1. Prepared by the gatekeeper, the assignment defines the problem and asks for solutions. When the responses are returned, the gatekeeper organizes the responses into a small number of categories.

2. The gatekeeper summaries the possible solutions offered by the re-spondents, who then are asked to indicate preferences in rank order.

3. The gatekeeper again summarizes the responses, including the pros

and cons of each. Participants then are asked for a final vote on the top three to five most popular suggestions.

4. The final vote is tabulated and revealed. This could culminate in a large group meeting to provide information and/or seek clarification. Or the results could simply be announced.

Delphi offers you an opportunity to get the opinions of a large number of people, as many as you wish. Participants feel involved and consulted, and you get their best collective opinion.

A disadvantage is the time the process consumes, during which nothing is happening. (Using e-mail can cut the time down appreciably.) Another disadvantage is the lack of spontaneity, something you have to give up if you really want to get the opinion of a medium or large group.

After using the Delphi technique to canvass opinion and to make a preliminary decision, you then can use other group methods to refine and improve the decision. For medium and large groups or when a group cannot get together, the Delphi technique is a powerful tool.

Putting Group Purpose and Group Size Together

Knowing group purpose and group size can make your group activities more effective. As the size and purpose of your group changes, so do group techniques. Smaller groups tend to be less complicated, while larger groups require more formal approaches. Figure 2 summarizes what you have learned about group size, group purpose, and medium-sized and large groups and gives you a road map to follow in plotting your strategy.

Giving Information. If you just want to give information, group size probably doesn't matter much. You may have to put some material in writing if it is highly complex, but essentially, few other changes in approach are needed, regardless of the group's exact size. Here is one of those few changes: as the group becomes larger, you'll need to formalize the procedure by asking people to write down their questions so that you can categorize and answer them. Nothing is very complex about this except, remember, the larger the group the more formal we must be, and the more we must prepare.

Giving and receiving information. Again, as the group size increases, the approach becomes more formal. With a small group, it's sufficient to share information, ask others to do the same, ask for questions, and then discuss how we can work together to help one another.

As the group gets larger (twelve or more), activities need to be more formal. Send out written materials in advance, and devote the meeting to answering questions about those materials. You can briefly discuss how group members can help one another, but it's deadly to have thirty people give their views—that can take up a day! Make them put it in writing.

As we move to thirty-one to sixty participants, formality becomes even more important. Rather than having a meeting, ask participants to provide in writing the information they want to share. If there is a meeting, it should involve summarizing what people have put in writing beforehand with time to discuss how people can help one another.

If the group is very big—over sixty—it must become even more formal. Perhaps you will need to break the meeting down into smaller groups.

Making decisions or advising a decision maker. Here different group sizes definitely require entirely different approaches. For small groups, you can get the group together to explore options, examine each option's advantages and disadvantages, have spirited discussion, and arrive at a decision. As the group gets larger, it must be more formal. You can use the consensus-seeking approach; the nominal group technique; and the Delphi approach, which, as you learned, is designed to lead larger groups to making decisions or recommendations.

You *can* get a decision from a large group! Just use the technique appropriate to the size. I have seen large groups arrive at good decisions where all felt involved in the process—even if they never got together. It can be done!

Developing new ideas and new approaches. Again, the method will change with size, but not as much as when making a decision. You can break large groups into small ones, using the same techniques. Later we will talk about brainstorming as a way to get groups to be creative.

Resolving differences. You learned a conflict resolution model that works well for resolving differences in groups with fewer than ten to fifteen participants. But modifications are necessary for larger groups. As you practice the techniques for dealing with medium-sized and large groups, the best approaches will become apparent.

Achieving understanding and acceptance of a decision. The strategy will

Figure 2. Effective Methods Based on Group Purpose and Group Size

Purpose	Size	Method
Give information	1	Remind self
	2–4	Short meeting; explain, answer questions
	5–11	Short meeting; explain, answer questions
	12–30	Short meeting; explain, answer questions
	31–60	Send letter or Web announcement; short meeting face to face or hold teleconference; explain, answer questions; don't deal with same question more than once
	61+	Send letter; do Web announcement; short meeting (if participants in different locations hold videoconference/use TV-satellite link); have people write questions, collect them, and deal with common themes at next meeting
Give and receive information	1	Meditate
	2–4	Short meeting; explain, answer questions; ask others for information; ask how group can help one another; summarize
	5–11	Short meeting; explain, answer questions; ask others for information; ask how group can help one another; summarize
	12–30	Share written materials; meet to answer questions (brief discussion as to how group can help one another)
	31–60	Share written materials; meet to answer questions or do over the Web; ask participants to provide suggestions later as to how others can help them
	61+	Share written materials; meet to answer questions or do over the Web; have members write in questions; have members write suggestions as to how others can help them.
Make decisions or advise a decision maker	1	Meditate
	2–4	Meet; explore options; arrive at a decision
	5–11	Meet; explore options; arrive at a decision
	12–30	Nominal group technique; consensus-seeking approach

Goal / Group size	Approach
31–60	Break large group into groups of 10 or more; use nominal group technique or consensus-seeking approach and then summarize findings
61+	Delphi approach; focus groups; break group down and use nominal technique or consensus-seeking approach
Develop new ideas, new approaches, leapfrog	
1	Meditate
2–4	Brainstorm or use nominal group technique
5–11	Brainstorm or use nominal group technique
12–30	Break into subgroups and brainstorm or use nominal group technique and summarize
31–60	Break into subgroups and brainstorm or use nominal group technique and summarize
61+	Same as above
Resolve differences	
1	Meditate, or flip coin?
2–4	Conflict resolution model learned
5–11	Conflict resolution model learned
12–30	Nominal group technique; Delphi approach; consensus-seeking approach
31–60	Delphi approach; subgroup use of conflict resolution model
61+	Delphi approach; subgroup use of conflict resolution model
Achieve understanding and acceptance of a decision	
1	Announce
2–4	Announce and discuss
5–11	Announce and discuss
12–30	Announce; anticipate questions and answer in formal remarks; take questions
31–60+	Announce (teleconference or over Web), anticipate questions and answer in formal remarks; have questions written out and handed in; answer a few according to themes presented

vary with group size. The larger the group and the more formal the activity, the more useful are mass communication techniques. (Here's where PR people can be very helpful.)

> *Reality Exercise.* Might some problem in your firm or in your church, student, or community group be resolved by a medium-sized or large group approach? What is it? Think through how you would use our approaches to move the group to agreement.

Positive and Negative Group Roles

Whether or not you are the chosen leader, you can greatly influence the outcome of group activities. You can make a great contribution, in substance and by enhancing group cohesion. In effect, you can be a leader—you can have the power that goes with leadership in areas where few people are skilled.

First, I will describe positive group roles and give examples. After that, I will describe negative influences—distractions created by those who work against group goals—and show how to deal with them. This will form the background for the next topic: how to run an effective meeting.

Positive Group Roles

Initiating. Getting things started; proposing a task be done; defining a problem; suggesting a procedure; getting the ball rolling:

"As I see it, what we need to do is identify options. I'll start with one and I hope others will follow."

"Why don't we try brainstorming as a way of getting some ideas? Joe, could you lead us?"

"Each of us is going to have to assume some responsibility for organizing the staff picnic—let's list the tasks and get volunteers. Areas not volunteered for will be filled in by lot."

"Our problem is that everyone wants to come to meetings, but no one wants to work on projects. Perhaps we should disband the group or agree to accept our share, perhaps change our goals."

Initiating is important. It gets things going and provides direction. Initia-

tors become leaders. There are many ways to initiate, such as writing a position paper or doing homework on a new approach. Taking initiative gives you
the edge. You influence. The group moves.

Information or opinion seeking. Most of us don't do this. We want to let
everyone know how we feel. Instead, we should be requesting facts and opinions from others, asking for suggestions or reactions:

"Joe, you're in investments. Is the stock market good for our group, and
should we invest in it at this time?"

"Marlene, I'd like to know your opinion on the proposal to disband the
group. How do you feel?"

"Let's hear Bill's response on the subject before deciding. He works in this
area."

This function is important because it allows everyone to participate. It
helps clarify issues (often people don't understand, but they don't say anything
because they are embarrassed). And it gets the group out of the rotation
process of speaking (taking turns). You become a leader because people like to
be asked what they think. Good leaders ask.

Summarizing. Stating your understanding of what was said or agreed to.
Summarizers put together ideas by restating them and by offering a decision
or conclusion for the group to accept or reject:

"Joe, I heard you saying that perhaps the stock market isn't stable enough
for us to invest in at this time" (restating).

"If I can combine several ideas heard this morning, perhaps we should:
(1) all agree to be here on time; (2) pay a twenty-five-cent penalty for every five
minutes late; (3) agree to give ten hours to each project; and (4) elect future
leaders."

"Let me see if I can summarize what the group seems to be saying to see if
we can arrive at a consensus: we have three choices—quit, work, or continue
99 percent fooling around."

Let's say a church group in its first ten minutes decides to have a fund
drive. They get off track and get back thirty minutes later to the same discussion: "As I recall, we already decided that" (summarizing); "Let's get on to
something else" (initiating).

Why? This helps the group reach closure (and closure is difficult to get).
It gets people on track and keeps them from rambling on. It reminds the group

of what has been said and in, some cases, what has been concluded. (Groups often forget and go back over the same territory.)

Standard-setting. The standard setter suggests rules that the group should adhere to:

"Could we set a group standard that all arrive at 7:30?"

Why? Standard setting defines rules that help focus the group.

Meeting socioemotional needs. Relieving tensions and encouraging people by being warm and friendly—all of which helps group members feel good and identify with the group:

"I like your suggestions."

"Let's take a break and relax. We're anxious to hear about your trip."

"I really enjoy being with you on Wednesdays."

"Fred, I like the way you are beginning to speak up. You have some great ideas."

"This group is really great—it's fun to be here."

If group needs aren't met, it won't stay together, especially in hard times. If you play a strong role in meeting the participants' needs, you will help to keep the group together and be influential yourself.

Reinforcing Good Behavior

How do you reinforce positive group behavior?

Be a good example. As you utilize positive group roles, others are encouraged to follow your lead. But don't always be the one to take the initiative; give others an opportunity to lead.

Evaluate. Spend five minutes at the end of the meeting assessing what was decided and how the group has performed:

"I am especially pleased that several of you attempted to summarize where we were. That really helped us stay on target."

"Bill's willingness to remind us that we shouldn't be too serious is greatly appreciated."

"I'm really glad that some of you invited others to present their ideas. We're much better off when everyone tells us how he or she feels. Our final decision will be better, and we'll all feel better about it."

"I really appreciate the way several of you took initiatives when we were stuck—you helped us get back on track."

It's always important to end by talking about the good things, reminding the participants of the importance of their work.

Identifying and Dealing with Negative Group Roles

Although we won't spend much time with these roles (I don't want you to learn them), you should be familiar enough with them so that you can spot them and do something about them.

Aggression. Belittling the acts of others: "You are a fool"; "Your idea is awful."

Recognition seeking. Boasting of personal achievements: "I had that idea years ago."

Dominating. Interrupting, manipulating: "I've got a better idea"; embarrassing others; flattering others to keep attention on oneself.

Blocking. Negativism or resistance beyond reason; even though the idea has been discounted ten times, refusing to let go: "I still believe we should yada yada."

Playboy. Kidding; noninvolvement; coming late.

Clinging vine. Seeking sympathy or understanding through depreciation of oneself (less a problem in work groups).

So, what do you do about the negative when you see it? During the summary period, avoid personal references while using it as an occasion to talk about the need for improvement:

"Seems to me we're horsing around too much; we find ourselves getting off track. Also, we need to start on time, which means everyone must be here on time."

"We seem to spend too much time belittling the ideas of others. Let's focus on the pros and cons of each idea. Let's avoid it being personal."

"We need more participation from the group—several seem to be dominating the group. This isn't good for them, and it isn't good for the final product."

Some suggestions can wait until after the main meeting, but some problems need to be dealt with as they happen.

Belittling. "Let's avoid the personal. Our task at hand is ya da ya da."

Dominating or blocking. Use your group skills to move the offender(s) over to another role.

If the *playboy* is acting up, get back to the subject. If he/she can be ignored, do so.

If someone's behavior continues to be disruptive, discuss it with him in private. Attempt to find out why. Let him know group parameters. If he continues to be a problem, seek to remove him.

But what if the group isn't working? What if no one knows how to be in a group, even if you are the best possible leader? You have a sick group! You could disband. Maybe the purpose isn't well understood. Maybe people don't know how to perform their group roles. Maybe they are intentionally sabotaging. In the absence of group skills, you might try bringing in a consultant to teach the members how to use positive skills and to identify and deal with negative group roles. But just maybe, this dysfunctional group needs to be shut down!

> *Self-Awareness Exercises.* 1. Which positive group roles are you best at? Pick one you'd like to improve and mentally rehearse how you will use it. Then use it and reflect on how things went.
>
> 2. Have you witnessed the negative roles being played in any groups? If so, mentally rehearse how you might deal with them. Prepare yourself for confronting negative roles being played by a fellow group member.

Running a Meeting

Most meetings aren't successful. But now your chances of being successful are greater—because you know about group size, group tasks, and the importance of purpose, and you are beginning to develop group skills. Already, you are way ahead of most!

When I was president of the University of Wisconsin system, we learned that there were over two hundred system meetings being held each year, with faculty and staff coming from all over the state to attend. We sent a questionnaire asking participants what they thought about the meetings. Were they necessary? If necessary, were they effective? If not, why not?

From this information we made a few changes. We eliminated some groups entirely, and we conducted many more meetings through conference calls. We also decided to help committee chairs develop better meeting-management skills.

The result was the development of a guide for chairing meetings, written by Elizabeth Schoenfeld. It was given to all chairs, and others read it through our quarterly house organ. Here are these simple rules modified for your purposes:

Preparation: Think

1. Define the meeting's general purpose. From what you've learned, decide what you want to accomplish: give information; give and receive information; advise a decision maker; develop new ideas (new approaches, e.g., leapfrogging the competition); resolve differences; or achieve understanding and acceptance of a decision. You should ask yourself the purpose each and every time you approach a meeting, to provide focus for your planning. Be mindful that meeting can have several purposes, depending on the issue being discussed.

2. Determine the meeting's specific goals. For example, if the group's general purpose is to make decisions or advise a decision maker, then what is to be decided this time? Know the specific goals and be ready to articulate them. Perhaps it is development of an employee reward system. Perhaps it's four or five major issues that you discussed before that now require closure.

3. Before proceeding further, ask "Is this meeting really necessary?" Sometimes it is not, sometimes the issues aren't ripe for development, sometimes the right people can't be there, sometimes it is too expensive to get people together, and sometimes there is not enough time. Sometimes the meeting is necessary, but it can be done through teleconferencing.

4. If a meeting is to be held, send materials out in advance. They should include the items to be discussed and the approximate time line (people like to know how long they'll be there). Also, include information reminding them of the desired outcome for each item—to share ideas, reach a decision, etc. For some important topics, talk with participants individually beforehand to give them a more in-depth understanding of areas to be discussed.

Conducting the Meeting

1. Always start the meeting on time. Don't wait more than five minutes for latecomers; willingness to wait may reinforce tardiness and redefine the actual meeting time. It also penalizes the conscientious and destroys group cohesion.

2. Begin by stating the purpose of the meeting, remind participants of the time line, and begin moving through the agenda.

3. If formal minutes need to be approved, ask for any changes or comments, but don't go into the issues again.

4. Follow the agenda, but be willing to move things around for group convenience. It is generally wise to take one or two easy issues first (to give the group confidence), then hit them with the hard issues (while they're still fresh), and close with other less difficult ones.

5. For each issue, provide its history, suggest a range of possible solutions, and point out any constraints.

6. Use the group skills mentioned earlier (initiating, information or opinion seeking, summarizing, standard setting, meeting socioemotional needs, etc.) to move participants to agreement.

7. Keep the discussion moving toward a group conclusion, but don't let the group rush to premature decisions. Look at all sides of an issue and examine consequences.

8. At the end of the discussion, recapitulate decisions and conclusions reached and be sure assignments are understood.

9. Finally, critique the proceedings.

Reality Exercise. 1. What are the biggest group errors you've seen in meetings? How might they be fixed?

2. Identify a meeting you will be chairing. Describe in writing how you will prepare for and conduct the meeting. If you're not scheduled to chair a meeting, make one up.

Creativity

Leading groups to greater creativity is rarely an easy task. We don't seem equipped to think this way. Most of the time, clear, logical thinking is sufficient, and thinking like everyone else is okay. But getting consensus is hard enough without throwing in demands for creativity. When you want creative ideas for such goals as beating the competition, different skills and mindsets are required. I told you at the start of this chapter that groups—if handled correctly—can be creative, sometimes more so than individuals. The method is simple, and it works in many cases. It can result in a *creative shift*—a new way of thinking, a major change in an existing approach, or an insight that goes far beyond current ideas.

Here are some ground rules:

1. Rule out evaluation (difficult). Encourage all participants to express their views. Do not allow judgmental comments, because evaluation will stifle the creative process. Our education has taught us to evaluate but not to create. We must quiet the silent judge that is always hovering nearby. No evaluation yet. Just ideas.

2. Encourage wild ideas and spontaneity. Nothing is stupid. Many significant inventions were someone's harebrained idea. The Wright Brothers, Alexander Bell—they had really stupid ideas, didn't they? Certainly the creators of the Internet should have known that it would never catch on! All ideas are encouraged, even the "very bad" ones.

3. Emphasize quantity, not quality. Ten good ideas out of a hundred are better than one out of ten.

4. Focus on one issue at a time. Clearly define the issue you face. If you define it too generally, you won't get good ideas. For example, "improving human relations" is too general. "Getting kids to stop fighting in school" is more specific.

5. Don't sell or explain. State suggestions as quickly as possible. Overselling ruins creative time. Just get it out.

6. Insist that all members participate. Everyone has good ideas. We need ideas. One idea from a usual nonparticipant might be the one that works best.

7. Record ideas.

8. "Hitchhike." Add to or subtract from previous ideas.

9. Discuss the recorded ideas.

10. Then, and only then, determine the best solutions. Up to this point, you have allowed your group to get outside itself by setting aside judgments. You now can get back to reality. Now you can arrive at the best solutions by using the nominal group technique, or the consensus-seeking approach.

This creative process can be a very powerful tool if you simply remember that sometimes suspending judgment is important.

Here is what you've learned to spur your group to creativity:
- Rule out evaluation
- Encourage wild ideas
- Emphasize quantity, not quality
- One problem at a time
- No selling or explaining
- Make all participate
- Record ideas
- "Hitchhike"
- Categorize recorded ideas and discuss
- Determine best solution(s)

Reality Exercise. Consider a problem you want to resolve. Prepare for a group brainstorming session. Find a place to try it, perhaps a class. Try it, then evaluate how it went. Think about how you can be even more effective next time.

6

Diversity

International Views of Leadership

Just when you thought that you knew how to be a better leader, I'm going to throw a wrench in the works that might complicate things: Leadership isn't alike in all cultures. Just as we learned earlier that individuals motivate themselves in different ways, different cultures are even more varied and complex.

A classic joke illustrates the point: In Britain, everything is permitted except what is forbidden; in Germany, everything is forbidden except what is permitted; and in France, everything is permitted, even what is forbidden. An obvious generalization, but you get the point. Even the definition of leader carries different historical, cultural, and public connotations. From Hoppe we learn that in ancient China, a leader was expected to be supremely cultured and educated—an accomplished scholar-administrator who, through extensive studies and rigorous exams in poetry, morality, philosophy, and the like, earned the privilege and duty of helping to run the country and its institutions.[1] Some remnants of that concept remain in today's China.

Hoppe tells us that the German experience under Hitler is a more recent example. His adoption of the name Führer (literally, leader) has greatly sullied the term *leader* in today's Germany.

Fortunately for us, there have been several outstanding studies and nu-

1. Michael Hoppe, "Cross-Cultural Issues in the Development of Leaders," in *The Center for Creative Leadership Handbook of Leadership Development*, 2d ed., ed. Cynthia D. McCauley, Ellen Van Velsor (San Francisco: Jossey-Bass, 2004).

merous interpretations of cultural similarities and differences. Most notably, Geert Hofstede[2] studied the differences in thinking and social action in more than fifty modern nations. House et al.,[3] under the Globe Research Program, studied more than sixty nations. Neither of these books, nor interpretations provided by others for that matter, makes for easy bedroom reading. But I will try to describe Hofstede's approach with the understanding that I'm trying not to make you an expert but to open your mind to the cultural differences that indeed exist, which can be systematically examined to determine if they influence approaches to leadership. Whether you agree with the findings of Hofstede and others is not important. What is important is to use his paradigm, or others, to better understand cultures that we might encounter. It *is* a small world.

2. Geert Hofstede, *Cultural Consequences*, 2d ed. (Thousand Oaks, Calif.: Sage, 2001).

3. House et al., *Culture, Leadership and Organizations.*

The Work of Geert Hofstede

Hofstede's groundbreaking work, involving 115,000 participants in fifty countries, laid the foundation for a better understanding of the importance of culture. He began by analyzing culture from four dimensions and later added a fifth. In this section, I will describe those five dimensions and show some cross-cultural comparisons. As you read, keep in mind that it is impossible to infer *individual* behavior from the cultural practices of a given group. Within each group exists a great variety of behaviors, just as you would find in a normal population distribution.

Hofstede argues that people are endowed with "mental programs"— developed in the family in early childhood and reinforced in schools and organizations—that contain an important component of national culture. The five dimensions that help to describe a group's culture are:

Power distance. This is the extent to which the less powerful members of organizations and institutions accept and expect that power is distributed unequally. In a "low power distance" culture, parents treat children as equals; in a "high power distance" culture, parents teach children obedience. In the work setting, cultures with a low power distance index (PDI) tend to decentralize decision making, concentrating less on authority, and relying more on personal experience and on subordinates. The ideal boss is a resourceful democrat who sees himself as practical and orderly and more reliant on support. Work organizations in a high PDI culture more likely have central decision-making structures, more concentration of authority, tall organization pyramids, and more reliance on formal rules.

Low PDI cultures frown upon managerial privileges and status symbols and are more comfortable with more equality. High PDI cultures respect managerial privileges and status symbols and are more comfortable with different valuations being attached to different jobs. Austria, Denmark, New Zealand, and Sweden have lower PDIs, while Malaysia, the Philippines, Mexico, Taiwan, and Japan have higher PDIs.

Uncertainty avoidance. This is the extent to which a culture programs its members to feel uncomfortable or comfortable in unstructured situations. The basic issue is the degree to which a society tries to control the uncontrollable. Rules help to protect against uncertainty, and the stronger a culture's tendency to avoid uncertainty, the greater its need for rules and the higher its uncertainty avoidance index (UAI). Some countries with high UAI values are Greece, Portugal, Salvador, Japan, France, and Chile. Countries with the lowest UAIs are the United States, India, Great Britain, Ireland, Hong Kong, Denmark, Jamaica, and Singapore.

Individualism and collectivism. This is the degree to which individuals are supposed to look after themselves or to be integrated into groups, usually around the family. In some cultures, individualism is regarded as a blessing and a source of well-being. In others, it is seen as alienating. Countries with high individualism value indexes (IDV) include the United States, Australia, Great Britain, France, and Denmark. Those with lower IDV values are Korea, Taiwan, Pakistan, and a number of Latin American countries. (By the way, many Arab countries seem to be grouped near the middle on this and other dimensions, which is why they haven't been mentioned.)

Masculinity and femininity. Here Hofstede refers to the distribution of emotional roles between the sexes, which he believes are fundamental issues for any society. He calls this the MAS index. I thought about leaving this dimension out because it appears so sexist, but it is one of the dimensions he uses, and if you read what he has to say, you would feel better about its use. He states that almost universally, women seem to attach more importance to social goals, such as relationships, helping others, and the physical environment, while men attach themselves more to ego goals such as careers and money (higher MAS values). Hoppe[4] gets us out of this dilemma by using the terms *tough* and *tender* rather than *masculine* and *feminine*. Tough cultures value challenging tasks, work and career, and competition. Tender cultures value cooperation, solidarity, and good relationships, as well as the quality of all aspects of life. Choose what term you will (I like tough and tender), but it would be disingenuous of me not to include a discussion of this dimension.

On Hofstede's scale, Japan, Austria, Venezuela, Italy, Mexico, Great Britain, Germany, Jamaica, and the Philippines scored highest on the tough side of the index. Lowest were the Scandinavian countries, Yugoslavia, South Korea, and Chile. On this dimension, the United States leans toward the tough side but is not as high as those I mentioned.

4. Michael H. Hoppe, "An Interview with Geert Hofstede," *Academy of Management* 18, no. 1 (2004): 1.

Long-term versus short-term orientation. This is the extent to which a culture programs its members to accept delayed gratification of their material, social, and emotional needs. Countries with a high long-term orientation (LTO) index were mainly in Asia and Southeast Asia. Countries with the lowest LTO orientation were Pakistan, Nigeria, Zimbabwe, and then, about in the middle, are the United States and Great Britain.

What does this information tell us? Not exactly what to expect in a given culture. It does tell us, however, that there are ways to examine different cultures. If we are thrust into an intercultural leadership position and ignore cultural differences, we will be operating at a great disadvantage. You can use Hofstede's paradigm, or someone else's, such as Hoppe's. The important thing is to have a way of looking at different cultures. Then, through reading and personal observation, you can begin to form opinions about how to work with your new friends. Keep in mind that this only explains group tendencies, not individuals.

Reality Exercises. 1. Using Hofstede's five dimensions, describe the culture in the United States.

2. If you're from another country, or have spent much time in another country, describe its culture using Hofstede's dimensions.

3. Pick a country other than the United States and learn about its culture, then develop a battle plan for how you would deal with your new friends in a leadership setting. How would it be similar to dealing with people in the United States? How would it be different?

U.S. Diversity: What Leaders Should Know

> *The only thing we know about the future is that it is going to be different.*
> — Peter Drucker, *The Essential Drucker*

> *As America becomes even more diverse, Army leaders are taught to be aware that they will deal with people from a wider range of ethnic, racial, and religious backgrounds. They are expected to appreciate beliefs different from their own as long as those beliefs don't*

conflict with Army values, are not illegal, and are not unethical. They are encouraged to actively seek out opportunities to learn about people and cultures different from their own. It shows respect to seek to understand other people's background, see things from their perspective, and appreciate what's important to them.

> —Francis Hasselbein and General Eric K. Shinseki (retired), *Be—Know—Do: Leadership in the Army*

Companies cannot afford the luxury of bias. They have to play the talent game to win.

> —Carly Fiorina, former president and CEO, Hewlett-Packard

You plan to work and live in this country and interact with just "plain old Americans," so why bother to learn about diversity issues? First, as you learned earlier, we are a global village now. Second, if you *could* manage never to be involved with people from other nations, you would still need to live and work in the United States—one of the most diverse countries in the world. And while we now are highly diverse, we'll be even more so in the future:

• By 2050, the U.S. population is expected to increase by 50 percent, and minority groups will make up nearly half the population, according to the U.S. Census Bureau. Immigration will account for almost two-thirds of the nation's population growth.

• U.S. Hispanic populations continue to grow at a much faster rate than the population as a whole. According to the bureau, the Hispanic population reached nearly 40 million on July 1, 2003, accounting for about one-half of the 9.4 million residents added to the nation's population since the 2000 census.

• The number of Asians, now exceeding 13 million, has grown by over 63 percent since the 2000 census. They now are America's fastest-growing group.

• Other kinds of diversity bring with them different viewpoints. There are female/male viewpoints (we're told that men are from Mars and women are from Venus). We see the emergence of gay and lesbian rights and its impact on the workplace and a societal concern for mainstreaming the disabled, in schools and at work.

• In the near future, the workplace will consist of four generations: (1) veteran, mature, and individualist—the senior; (2) Boomers, born after the end of World War II; (3) Generation X, born between 1965 and 1978, and (4) Generation Y (millennials) born after 1978. Each generation has its own points of view on civic engagement and the importance of work.

If you want to lead in this highly diverse world and a global economy, you must be able to work with people from all walks of life. From a purely selfish standpoint, no business—no country, for that matter—can afford not to use its entire pool of qualified people. This is one reason we were ahead of the game during the Internet revolution. The influx of foreigners to our universities and workplaces did much to help us leapfrog ahead of the competition. Consider: The foreign-born account for more than half of the engineers with doctorates working in the United States, and 45 percent of the nation's computer science doctorates. Children of immigrants constitute 65 percent of the top scorers in the 2004 U.S. Math Olympiads and 46 percent of the U.S. Physics Team.

I can't expect you to be knowledgeable about every possible diversity situation. But I can provide you with some basic principles, with the expectation that it will fuel your desire to grow and know more, as your reading and situations require. In this section, I'm providing the views of colleagues who have much to say about the topic. Special insights regarding African Americans, women, and gays and lesbians will be included. I apologize for not including more, but my purpose is to open your mind, not to give you a primer on every aspect of diversity. Much of what is provided pertains to the workplace but can be generalized to other situations.

Before these special features, however, I want to begin with my views regarding the levels of dealing with diversity. They are: (1) understanding discrimination laws, (2) having tolerance for others, (3) appreciating others, and (4) identifying and tearing down institutional barriers. Consider these as stages of development. Your diversity IQ score is highest when you can do all four. Obviously, if you achieve a low score you need to do a lot of reading and soul searching.

Discrimination. Many forms of discrimination are illegal. Today, federal and state laws, most notably the civil rights acts and the establishment of affirmative action, give us legal guidance. It is unlawful to prevent someone from buying a house, voting, or using public accommodations or to discriminate in the workplace. Most employers provide information about antidiscrimination laws; a good leader knows these laws well. Corporations that ignore discrimination laws find themselves in major trouble. Consider the recent travails of Merrill Lynch, Morgan Stanley, and Mitsubishi. As I write this, Wal-Mart is involved in what may be the largest lawsuit yet, stemming mostly from alleged violations of women's rights. A good leader doesn't need to be an expert on legal discrimination but needs to know enough to stay out of serious trouble and to ensure that others do, too.

Tolerance. This is the ability to respect both the differences and the similarities of people we work and live with. An effective leader can "do business" with anyone at any time. You don't have to like everybody, but it is essential that the business at hand be carried out with civility and respect for all parties. If you can't do this, you'll find yourself excluded from the table where the real action is.

Appreciation. This is a step up from just knowing the rules and being tolerant. The person who appreciates others does more than follow the law and exercises tolerance. He has developed the capacity to find value in everyone and to capitalize on what they can add to the mix. In our highly demanding world, it is easier to prejudge others—for example, to say that women are emotional and men are overly logical—rather than to learn about and truly appreciate others who are not exactly like us. People sense when you really appreciate them, and they sense when you don't.

Institutional barriers. The leader who has reached this level looks for barriers that impede the development of others and attempts to ameliorate and, in some cases, eliminate them. Remember, we can't afford to diminish our labor pool by excluding. We need the most able and motivated to be competitive in this world economy. What are examples of institutional barriers? One barrier for many employed mothers with small children is fixed work hours. Daycare helps. Flexible working hours—flextime—also could assist these mothers, who are expected to work as long and as hard as everyone else. A similar adjustment would allow employees to work at home. Again, this not a way to lighten the workload, but a way to maximize productivity. Another example is how key corporate decisions are discussed after golf in men's locker rooms.

Women and probably many minorities would be excluded from these critical exchanges, regardless of their formal job titles. The solution is to ensure that workplace decisions are made where those who need to be involved can participate.

The elimination of institutional barriers is no easy task, and no one size fits all solutions. But being sensitive to their possible existence helps you to better take advantage of everyone's strengths.

Let's hear from several people who have agreed to share their insights with you. First, Jeff Unaitas will tell us what it means to be a gay professional and what we can do as leaders to make our workplaces more hospitable to gays. Then, Barry Wells will give us insights into the African American experience.

FROM A GAY PROFESSIONAL: What Leaders Should and Probably Already Do Know | Jeff Unaitis[5]

"I'm gay."

With that declaration, the way you view me as son or daughter, husband or wife, mother or father, friend or neighbor, boss or coworker, changes irrevocably.

It shouldn't. It usually does.

I've said those words many times in my life and will, undoubtedly, say them again as I move through personal, social, and professional situations. It's not a difficult acknowledgment for me anymore, but it's enough for some to change their opinions about my fitness and ability to work alongside them, to be their friend or supervisor. I don't take that pronouncement lightly—never have—and yet I've only begun to appreciate its significance in helping to change the perceptions of those I work with and for. In fact, I consider it a responsibility.

It's 2005, and some might argue that there has never been a better time for the GLBT employee in the workplace (GLBT is the common acronym for "gay, lesbian, bisexual, and transgender"; for purposes of this essay, I'll use "gay" as an inclusive adjective for all these descriptors). Great strides have been made in recognizing, recruiting, retaining, and rewarding gay employ-

5. Jeff Unaitis is Vice President, Public Affairs, Time Warner Cable Syracuse Division, and has been active as a leader in a variety of local and statewide activities.

ees on a level equal with their coworkers, a reflection of an increasing accept-ance, I believe, by the larger community.

The mass media is more accurately reflecting the lives of gay men and women on television and in film. Mass marketers have (apparently overnight) recognized the buying power of the gay population and targeted these con-sumers through campaigns in gay-oriented publications and other advertising channels. There are new and planned gay cable networks. Colleges and uni-versities have gay fraternities. Even the evolution of the "metrosexual"—the heterosexual male who cares about skin care, style, and fashion—is a nod to the increasing acceptance of the so-called "gay lifestyle."

For many of us (but not all), there is no longer the oppressive shame or stigma once associated with identifying ourselves as gay. The "coming-out" process, while still a highly personal and challenging milestone of self-awareness, is made easier today by the experiences of those who have fought long and hard before us for acceptance and understanding. The modern gay rights movement in the United States recognizes its origins at the Stonewall Riots in New York City in 1969. In only thirty-five years, then, we're talking about full workplace equality. We've come a long way . . . but why do we even need to have this discussion?

I like to believe—want to believe—that everybody today is acquainted with a gay coworker, knows a gay neighbor, has a gay friend, accepts a gay fam-ily member—in short, that we live our lives side by side in openness and full equality.

Yet, at the dawn of the twenty-first century, it's clear we have a long way to go. Here's a snapshot of where we're at today:

• "Marriage in the United States shall consist only of the union of a man and a woman. Neither this Constitution or the constitution of any State, nor state or federal law, shall be construed to require that marital status or the legal incidents thereof be conferred upon unmarried couples or groups" (Federal Marriage Amendment, defeated, at least as of this writing, by both the U.S. House of Representatives and Senate); "Legal recognition and the accompa-nying benefits afforded couples should be preserved for that unique and spe-cial union of one man and one woman, which has historically been called marriage" (excerpt from the 2004 national platform of the Republican Party). The evolution of the gay marriage debate dominated headlines and campaign speeches during 2004, with some successes but many more setbacks; a political party expressly advocates for the denial of equal benefits for gay couples.

• The Employment Non-Discrimination Act (ENDA), a gay civil rights bill granting workplace protections to gay workers, has been stalled in Congress for more than ten years.

• "Don't Ask/Don't Tell/Don't Pursue/Don't Harass" remains U.S. military policy, resulting in the discharge of more than ten thousand otherwise qualified individuals since 1993. Significantly, the number of linguists in the military discharged because they are gay is growing, according to statistics maintained by the Servicemembers Legal Defense Network, despite a critical need for language specialists in the so-called "War on Terror." According to a Government Accounting Office (GAO) study released in January 2002, the army faces a critical shortfall in linguists needed to translate intercepts and interrogate suspected terrorists, and concluded that staff shortfalls "have adversely affected agency operations and compromised U.S. military, law enforcement, intelligence, counterterrorism and diplomatic efforts."

Against that devastating backdrop of politics and policy run amuck, the workplaces and workers of America have distinguished themselves by actively recognizing their roles in advancing their employees and coworkers based on performance, not on some irrelevant personal aspect of their lives. The times are changing. The signs are increasingly positive:

• The Human Rights Campaign, the largest U.S. gay, lesbian, bisexual and transgender advocacy organization, released its 2004 Corporate Equality Index, its annual (since 2002) survey of how major U.S. corporations treat their gay employees, consumers, and investors. In 2004, a total of fifty-six companies received a perfect score of 100—more than four times the number of perfect scores in 2002. The HRC credits its annual review with spurring the acceptance and creation of gay-friendly workplace policies, protections, and benefits.

• According to a 2004 Out & Equal Workplace Summit survey, conducted by Harris Interactive in conjunction with Witeck-Combs Communications, more than half of heterosexuals (55 percent) feel that married spouses and same-sex partners should receive the same adoption assistance, such as counseling and financial benefits, offered by many employers. Seven in ten (70 percent) heterosexuals agree that the leave rights for family and medical emergencies (as outlined in the Family and Medical Leave Act) should apply equally to employees' married spouses and to same-sex partners.

• That same survey showed a majority of heterosexuals believe that same-sex partners of employees should be treated equally for workplace benefits that are usually extended automatically to the married spouses of employees, including tax-free health insurance benefits (67 percent), health insurance coverage under COBRA when an employee leaves a job (66 percent), relocation expenses when a spouse/partner is transferred by his or her employer (65 percent), and leave benefits for employees who experience the loss of a spouse/partner or close family member (78 percent).

In the United States, then, it's clear that the private sector is taking the lead in opening up its workplaces to employees regardless of their sexual or affectational preferences, without mandate or even encouragement by our governments. In a competitive capitalistic economy, I suppose that's the way it should be. That makes our roles as leaders even more essential to nurturing and advancing all our employees, because we recognize it's the right thing to do: it's the only thing to do.

I'm fortunate to work for both an employer and a boss who have made the acceptance of employees based on performance more important than any personal attribute or characteristic. We're fighting to get and keep customers, fighting to get and keep the best employees. The fact that I'm gay has and should have no bearing on my ability to perform my job, nor should any personal or familial relationship color my perception of any other employee's ability to perform his or her job.

In fact, I suggest that my empathies, developed around my personal attributes and experiences, give me a unique advantage in understanding and appreciating the diversity of the people I work with and for, and the customers we serve. My company recognizes that; my boss values that. Many of my gay friends are envious because their own employers have yet to see the benefits of embracing all they can and do willingly offer. I encourage them to keep fighting for that acceptance.

While I don't consider myself a minority in the traditional sense of that word (although I most certainly am), I'm consistently and consciously aware of the differing viewpoints and concerns that emanate from our varied life experiences. I willingly and enthusiastically bring my own differences to the table and am not afraid to share my perspectives as a gay man. I similarly expect and encourage other employees to speak and share from their experiences. A good employer and better leader is one who encourages, values, and appreciates those differences.

On the contrary, gay employees who feel threatened in the workplace, who are subject to or feel subject to harassment, who are under constant pressure to hide and deny this integral part of their lives — can't be employees performing at the top of their game. Who does that hurt most?

For example, at my company we evaluate employees annually on their integrity (along with other more quantitative workplace indicators). If the environment doesn't allow employees to live and share their lives honestly, how can we expect them to similarly embrace our other organizational objectives? What are we saying about what matters most? Where is *our* integrity?

Although I have never found it necessary to deny my sexual orientation, I would expect that the physical, mental, and psychic toll on employees who feel it necessary, in order to succeed, to create a sham "straight" life would ultimately affect their day-to-day workplace performance. The employer then loses the full abilities and dedication of those employees, where we should be interested in helping them to maximize their success without regard to non-employment issues or attributes. That's what real leaders do.

For employees who may be struggling with coming-out issues, we should be prepared to provide guidance and support to the best of our abilities. If the company offers its workers an Employee Assistance Program (EAP), we should feel confident in that referral program's abilities to provide counseling in the areas of self-identity and sexual orientation. Supervisors should be encouraged to attend sensitivity training or company-required diversity training, where sexual orientation is included and discussed openly.

Of course, a workplace must maintain and promote nondiscrimination and sexual harassment policies that include and encompass issues of sexual orientation and identification, and those policies must be enforced consistently and fairly in all employee situations. It's one thing to create, maintain, and promote a good policy. Employees (and potential employees) need to see policy in action if they are to feel protected and supported by the organization.

I'm a gay employee with a longtime partner, so I've used my relationship aggressively to pursue and promote concepts of fairness and equality arising from the company's employee benefits package. For example, while my company does offer health insurance to same-sex domestic partners, IRS regulations currently require the company's contributions to those premium payments be considered taxable income. It's not fair, but that's the law. I make sure that my organization's Human Resources Department recognizes that distinction for, although there's the sense that corporate America is moving in the right direction, we will only achieve equality and fairness when there are no more distinctions.

It's important for me, I believe, to challenge and cajole the company openly as it reviews and revises policies in an effort to ensure that all benefits are applied equally to all employees and their partners, regardless of legal or regulatory limitations imposed by current statute. You may not have a gay employee in a position of authority to force those reviews of policy and advocate for inclusiveness, so I encourage you to read and understand every applicable policy or benefit from the point of view of a gay employee.

Then, those of us in leadership positions must constantly encourage our employees to take advantage of the full range of benefits available to them. For example, when an employee acknowledges that he or she is gay and has a partner who is interested in enrolling in the company's insurance program, we should be pleased that the employee sees this as a further inducement to remain at our company. It wasn't long ago that some employees would fear such an admission as a career-jeopardizing announcement. With a shrinking labor pool of skilled, qualified applicants, it only makes good sense to retain and motivate your best employees by delivering on your full range of benefits—and some of your best employees are gay.

Beyond the benefits packages and policy manuals, though, your organization needs to evaluate day-to-day workplace issues to ensure that gay employees feel fully included and welcomed in the life of the company.

If employees bring in family photos to decorate their workspaces, do gay employees feel comfortable displaying pictures of their partners? Do gay employees bring their partners or a friend to company-sponsored picnics or parties? If the company sponsors a community activity or event, are gay employees similarly encouraged to attend with their partners? Does the company support gay-identified organizations in the community through cash donations or sponsorships?

If you aren't able to answer these and similar questions, there's an easy and effective solution: ask your gay employees! While larger companies may have an active and company-sponsored GLBT employee group, smaller companies probably don't. Offer to host an informal meeting of your gay employees and their allies in an effort to understand the unique conditions imposed by your workplace, with a goal of understanding ways in which the company can be more responsive to current shortcomings while creating opportunities for continuing dialogue. Word will get out both within and outside the organization that gay employees are recognized and valued. Your customers will appreciate that, and your employees will understand the importance the company places on an inclusive work environment.

I'm in a unique position, as the liaison between my company and the communities we serve, to set an example personally and for the company by contributing resources to organizations and activities that reach out to the gay community. We have actively supported our HIV/AIDS service organizations with contributions and promotional support, and I have chaired the local AIDS Task Force board of directors; we have provided program advertisements to the local Gay and Lesbian Chorus, part of a growing national movement of gay musical groups; my company sponsored a production at our local professional theater that was actively promoted to gay audiences. We don't and won't shy away from gay organizations or causes.

We do these things to show that we're involved with all aspects of our community, that we value every contribution made by the individuals and the variety of human service and cultural institutions that call this place home. We want current and future employees and customers to know that we're engaged and committed. I'm proud to say that we're not the only company that is increasingly lending its support and its name to a diversity of community groups that include gay-identified organizations. On a national scale, many Fortune 500 companies have also embraced gay causes and special events. There is almost certainly a bottom-line benefit to marketing to the gay community but, even more important, those companies have sent out the unmistakable signal that they appreciate their gay customers and employees.

Even with this progress, the move to acceptance necessarily begins with small steps. As leaders, we do what we can within our companies and organizations to move toward a more open society. Are all individuals going to be tolerant and supportive of an organization that chooses to acknowledge, without prejudice, its gay employees? Of course not. Although studies show that younger generations are generally more tolerant of gays and lesbians and supportive of workplace equality issues, there are still significant religious, political, and moral elements fighting against those same issues and, unfortunately, with some success.

If you recognize the benefits to your organization, to your employees who might be gay (or who have a gay sibling, or gay parent, or gay child), to your customers—then you know beyond a doubt that you must recognize and treat your gay employees as you would any employee.

I'm hopeful that increasing gay visibility, supported by growing trends in corporate recognition, acceptance, and acknowledgment are leading to a greater sensitivity and appreciation for gay employees in the workplace and our greater society.

That's what we, as leaders, should encourage and expect. [JEFF UNAITIS]

Barry Wells has insights from an African American perspective that you will find helpful.

ON COLOR AND LEADERSHIP | Barry L. Wells[6]

> *Mentoring is not necessarily a matter of color; rather, it
> is a matter of skill and commitment.*
> —Charles V. Willie

Leadership comes in many shapes and forms, with individuals in positions of power and influence possessing diverse personal qualities, unique backgrounds, and organizational styles based on their own life experiences. While today's leadership styles may vary, individuals in leadership roles are truly not diverse in terms of race and ethnicity, and consequently not in the related life experiences that ultimately shape their views, behaviors, and decisions in the workplace.

---

6. Barry L. Wells is Senior Vice President and Dean of Student Affairs at Syracuse University. In addition to his university responsibilities, he has been active in community initiatives and as a spokesman for students at the national level.

A quick perusal of the leadership team for any given organization, whether it is a multinational conglomerate, a government agency, or a private institution of higher education, will more often than not reveal a homogenous makeup that is typically white and male. The need to understand leadership is perhaps at an all-time high as organizations, and the individuals in them, focus on progress and change like never before, operating in complex, dynamic, and diverse global settings that are goal-driven, time- and resource-conscious, and results-oriented. National research geared toward organizational leaders repeatedly suggests that a diverse workforce encourages active and conscious thinking, which leads to success. That leads to the conclusion that the whole organization should be diverse, and those in leadership roles, too, should be from diverse backgrounds. Yet the reality suggests otherwise. America's boardrooms, for example, remain composed largely of white men.[7]

How then, do people of color reach their potential for leadership if they aspire to do so? Mentoring is one of the best ways to share knowledge and experience, and consequently, a viable solution for increasing opportunities for success for people of color in leadership positions. John Gardner, in his book *On Leadership*, explained that there is "much about leadership that is best learned from living examples."[8]

This essay will focus specifically on the challenges people of color aspiring to leadership roles face, with practical advice for reaching their goals, along with guidance for those who are white and interested in mentoring persons of color into leadership roles.

Obstacles to Leadership

Like their predecessors, men and women of color today are generally held to higher standards working in environments that are predominantly white, which is perhaps the most notable challenge they face in reaching their aspirations to lead. Although their performance should be assessed by the content of their work and not by the color of their skin, that's not what happens, even though many will argue society, as a whole, has made tremendous progress in

7. Julie Bennett, "For Women and Minorities, Reaching the Boardroom Remains a Rough Ride," *Wall Street Journal*, Oct. 12, 2004.

8. John Gardner, *On Leadership*.

the area of racial and ethnic equality. It has been historically difficult for persons of color to fulfill their leadership potential, for starters because of the obstacles they face, at times on a daily basis. These obstacles are certainly not circumstances that they played any role in creating, yet they are saddled with them inappropriately, which affects the opportunities they have for leadership because others have told them they aren't worthy or capable of leadership before they are given a fair chance to prove otherwise.

Unlike their counterparts whose skin is white, persons of color are constantly faced with dispelling the myth that they have gotten ahead in the workplace because of special treatment, based on the color of their skin and not the contributions they have made to the organization. The implication is that persons of color don't have the qualifications or intellect to lead. Despite an individual's continued record of demonstrated success, if he is a person of color, he will have to prove his skills and intellect repeatedly, in contrast to many of his white peers.

There is one story that immediately comes to mind to illustrate this point. Upon accepting a professorship at Harvard University following a very impressive twenty-five-year career at Syracuse University, Dr. Charles V. Willie, a sociologist who is currently the Charles William Eliot Professor of Education at the Harvard University Graduate School of Education, was approached by a white sociologist at the news of his appointment. Willie was shocked when this so-called friend offered not congratulations or best wishes, but instead, "I wish I were black." The implication was pretty clear—in this friend's eyes, this appointment was a result of race and not one of scholarly accomplishment. Another colleague, a white administrator at Syracuse University, shared a similar sentiment with the acknowledgment of his appointment: "I don't know whether I should congratulate you or envy you." Willie attributes the remark to this white colleague's feeling he was more deserving than Willie of the appointment.[9]

As a young African American boy attending a predominantly white parochial elementary school, I soon realized there were people out there who would judge a person solely by the color of his skin, especially if it was differ-

9. Charles V. Willie, *Effective Education: A Minority Policy Perspective* (New York: Greenwood Press, 1987).

ent from theirs and from that of the majority. In their brutal honesty, my white peers would confront me regularly using the N-word, or call me black, using the word in a taunting and hurtful manner. My mother, who grew up in the deep segregated South, taught me and my older brother never to accept such name-calling passively. She taught us to confront and challenge such ignorance and hate directly. She also taught us that we'd have to work harder than those around us whose skin was white. Moreover, if we were going to function in life, and certainly in the workplace, we'd need to understand that life wasn't always fair, especially for people of color. She was right. For a person of color who is in a leadership role today—and for people of color aspiring to a leadership role—it's great advice.

Scholars on leadership will agree it is no mystery that so many promising men and women of color never really maximize their potential and often fade without showing others what they really can do. Although ability and skill are critical to success, fulfilling one's promise is dependent on attributes outside of talent, such as courage, fortitude, and the ability to stay one's course despite obstacles.[10] These are the very issues mentors can help protégés navigate, yet the opportunities for persons of color to enlist the support and commitment of good mentors are, at times, limited. The time has come to provide promising leaders of all colors the camaraderie, guidance, and encouragement that mentorship provides.

Considerations for Persons of Color Aspiring to Leadership

Regardless of a person's color, he or she should develop an understanding of leadership—and specifically how different individuals fulfilled their promise to lead—through research, ongoing reading, obtaining mentors, and professional development on related topics. "Servant leadership" is one useful philosophy of leadership that helps individuals in both the minority and the majority grasp the role of power and politics in leadership, along with the differences between management and leadership. Perhaps most important in Robert Greenleaf's practical philosophy of servant leadership, which supports service first and leads to the conscious aspiration of leadership next, is whether

10. John Gardner, *On Leadership.*

those served grow as persons. And specifically, how does their leadership affect the least privileged in society—will they benefit, or, at least, will they not be further deprived?[11] Anyone aspiring to leadership, regardless of skin color, should pay close attention to the leadership styles of those at the top in molding their own personal behaviors. One can learn more about the skills necessary for leadership by observing good leaders than one can learn from a bad leader who demonstrates how *not* to lead by his or her poor example of questionable values, decisions, and motivations.

It is critical to gain an understanding of one's individual strengths, weaknesses, goals, and values as a human being. With a sense of these fundamentals identified, it is then easy to identify one's personal style. In his book *The Seven Habits of Highly Effective People,* Steven R. Covey describes ultimate success as "success with self," which comes from self-awareness. Covey encourages individuals to develop self-awareness as a way of discovering ineffective scripts of behavior and action that are not only inconsistent with who individuals are, but that get in the way of what they really value in life. It is easy to lose sight of values and goals in the day-to-day activity of life's immediate concerns, problems, and challenges both in the workplace and at home. Yet those who aspire to leadership, regardless of color, need to realize they are not to be limited in what they can achieve by their self-imposed obstacles any more than by those created by others.[12]

According to Covey, the most effective way to become self-aware is to develop a personal mission statement, identifying who you want to be and what you want to do, drawing significantly from your values. He compares personal mission statements to the United States Constitution, which as we know, has been virtually unchanged over two hundred years. It is a foundation. And it works. On personal mission statements, he writes: "Once you have that sense of mission, you have the essence of your own proactivity. You have the vision and the values which direct your life. You have the basic direction from which you set your long-term and short-term goals. You have the power of a written constitution based on correct principles, against which decisions concerning

11. Robert K. Greenleaf, *Servant Leadership: A Journey into the Nature of Legitimate and Greatness* (New York: Paulist Press, 1977).

12. Stephen R. Covey, *The 7 Habits of Highly Effective People* (New York: Simon and Schuster, 1989).

the most effective use of your time, your talents, and your energies can be effectively measured." [13]

While an individual's mission statement is a personal expression of direction and conviction, people of color aspiring to leadership can benefit significantly by affiliation with a mentor.

William E. Rosenbach is the Evans Professor of Eisenhower Leadership Studies and Professor of Management at Gettysburg College. He is the coauthor of *Contemporary Issues in Leadership*, which focuses on the effectiveness of leadership. He describes mentoring as "empowering followers to be leaders." Mentors open doors for mentees that might otherwise not be easy to open or ones that seemingly cannot be opened at all. Mentors provide support that helps followers arrive at good decisions through continuous support and feedback. A good mentoring relationship provides intellectual and emotional support that offers challenge and excitement, in addition to professional development and growth. The distinction between managers and leaders is perhaps best understood through the study of what many now call "transformational" leadership—when one person engages with others in such a way that the leader and the followers raise one another to higher levels of motivation and morality. In such cases, the leader, the follower, and the environment where they interact are transformed. [14]

My friend and esteemed colleague Dr. Willie, when asked about his personal experience with a mentor, shared the story of an offer he received for a research associate position at Syracuse University's Youth Development Center and also as an assistant professor in the Department of Sociology. At the time, he was an accomplished professional, having received his Ph.D. in 1957 and having eight years of teaching experience in higher education, along with seven articles published in professional journals. Intrigued—and very interested in the offer, he requested the rank of associate professor instead of assistant professor. He was denied this request because his former rank at the Upstate Medical Center was instructor. He was told one does not skip the rank above the one previously held.

With this denial, he then made a countersuggestion that he be granted

13. Covey, 7 *Habits*.

14. William E. Rosenbach and Robert L. Taylor, eds., *Contemporary Issues in Leadership* (Boulder, Colo.: Westview Press, 1993).

tenure as an assistant professor. The dean of the College of Liberal Arts at that time had been a mentor to him previously and interceded on his behalf, going to the highest levels of administration, which ultimately led to Dr. Willie's appointment as assistant professor of sociology with tenure. One might say this turn of events was quite unusual and unheard of. Willie is convinced to this day that the appointment was made because he had the confidence and courage to ask for it, but also because he had a mentor to support and advise him.

I've used the same approach for negotiating different job offers time and time again. My mentors have always taught me to be patient and thorough whenever I have been involved in such negotiations. They've advised me to think through the pros and cons of any offer, and also to use this time for negotiating counterrequests, since at this point in time, I am in the driver's seat.

Racism still exists today, even though it may not be as overt as it was a generation ago. Modern-day racism is perhaps more daunting and disturbing, as it appears covertly, often at the hands of crafty, calculating individuals working behind the scenes, who feel prejudice will bring them their fair share and then some. It is still true that positions of leadership in American society are dominated by white males. However, there are steps that leaders can take to create an environment for personal and professional accomplishment, satisfaction, and growth, with pathways to leadership for people of color.

Mentoring Persons of Color

Leaders of all colors need to recognize and acknowledge that racism does indeed exist. To deny it is to undermine the ability to lead, compromising the effectiveness of the organization and the people in it.

One doesn't have to be a person of color to mentor a person of color. In fact, mentoring a person of color is one of the key steps nonminorities in leadership positions can take. Case in point: renowned black historian John Hope Franklin was mentored by T. S. Courier, his white history professor at Fisk University. It was Courier who took out a personal loan to get Franklin through his first year of graduate school at Harvard.[15]

15. Charles V. Willie, *Black Issues in Higher Education*, May 15, 1988.

View the advice I offer to nonminorities who choose to mentor people of color as a good beginning, a starting point in developing effective and rewarding mentoring relationships. As this relationship develops, I have every confidence these mentees will tell their respective mentors what other things they should know.

First, nonminority mentors must be cautious not to say things such as, "I understand your experiences as a person of color." Unless you are a person of color yourself, you can't. That is not to say your experiences and knowledge do not offer valuable support to persons of color aspiring to be leaders; mentoring relationships, if they are to be productive, are two-way streets. The most important message mentors want to share is that they will do all they can to help mentees realize their potential by sharing what they know.

Dr. Willie, who has studied and written widely on mentoring methodologies for minorities, identifies three areas for leaders of any color who mentor people of color:

1. The mentor must first accept another person just the way she is before attempting to induce a change in her behavior.

2. The mentor must trust another if the other is ever to become trustworthy.

3. The mentor must support the mentee by sharing in her suffering, which is a source of security that enables people to succeed.[16]

Accept that the minority is unlike the majority, and work with those in the minority to accept this fact, too. Understand—and help them understand—that they should be who they are, not who they feel the organization, or society as a whole, expects them to be. It is the differences they bring to the table, along with the skills they possess, that make them an asset to any given organization.

Dr. Willie feels that breaking bread together is one of the best ways for a mentor to show acceptance and support for his or her mentee. When he was a graduate student at Syracuse University, he knew his mentor, who was his English professor as well, accepted him as he was and for who he was when he invited him to his home for dinner. Later, when the professor was critical of the first essay he handed in, the young student was able to accept the criticism

16. Willie, *Effective Education.*

of his writing because he knew the professor had already accepted him as a person. It was more than dinner—it was the securing of a bond of trust.[17]

In mentoring people of color, don't underestimate them or condescend to them. It represses productivity and does little, if anything, to build a relationship of trust and respect. Leaders must help people believe in what they can do—they can be effective, they can achieve their goals, and they can make the future better for themselves and for others like them. Leaders must take steps to remove the obstacles to excellence and the circumstances limiting people of color.

Earlier in this essay, we looked at self-awareness and the role it played for persons of color aspiring to leadership positions. Taking self-awareness one step further is the practice of empathy. In the book *Emotional Intelligence*, Daniel Goleman suggests that empathy builds on self-awareness. And he's right. The more one is able to understand one's self and one's emotions, the more skilled one becomes at reading the feelings and understanding the needs of others.[18] That ability—to read someone else and know how they are feeling—is critical for nonminorities.

In the book *The Leadership Challenge*, readers are advised to write their own credos. Authors James M. Kouzes and Barry Z. Posner assign the exercise of writing a one-page memo sharing the values and beliefs needed to guide action and decision making in your absence, somewhat like Covey's direction on the mission statement. If you haven't gone through a similar exercise, you might find this one beneficial to organizational understanding and ensuring the right values are in place in the workplace so that all persons, not just those of one skin color, can benefit.

Last, nonminority leaders must stick to the facts. Don't stereotype persons of color, pretending to know them by generalizations or preconceived notions. While refraining from stereotyping their personality traits because of the color of their skin, refrain as well from generalizing what you think their personal experiences have been. Take the time to learn about their individual experiences, their personal goals and aspirations, and their own views. True leaders understand that there are differences in cultures.

17. Willie, *Black Issues in Higher Education*.
18. Daniel Goleman, *Emotional Intelligence* (New York: Bantam Books, 1995).

Implications for the Future

Ask anyone in a position of leadership how they got where they are, and they will tell you the path they took to the top had as many challenges as it had rewards.

Certainly as a young boy, next a college student, and then a black professional aspiring to leadership, I had many mentors who had confidence in me. Without question, I placed my trust in them. Today, as a person of color in a leadership position on a university campus, I mentor both students and aspiring professionals who are persons of color, using the same formula of confidence and trust resulting in respect. Many of you have had different paths to your respective leadership positions, and more likely than not there has been at least one individual, if not more than one, who has showed you the way. If you've been fortunate, you've had the leadership and friendship of a good mentor. The essence of my parting message remains the same—mentoring can make a leadership difference. [BARRY L. WELLS]

Women in Leadership Positions

Yes, women are from Venus and men are from Mars, as Tannen[19] has suggested. Both research and our own common-sense observations confirm that. Komives,[20] for example, says many women and men find different reasons for their successes or failures. Women tend to credit such external factors as luck and being in the right place at the right time. They attribute their failures to such personal factors as being unprepared or lacking the right skills. In contrast, many men tend to credit their success to such personal factors as being prepared and capable, while blaming their failures on such external factors as fate, other peoples' failings, or just plain old bad luck.

Tannen describes a study in which researchers eavesdropped on the conversations of women and men bank professionals. When no women were present, the men talked most often about business, then food and sports, in that

19. Deborah Tannen, *You Just Don't Understand: Women and Men in Conversation* (New York: Ballentine Books, 1991).

20. Komives, Lucas, and McMahon, *Exploring Leadership*.

order. They never talked about people. When women talked alone, their most frequent topic was people—not people at work so much as friends, children, and partners in personal relationships. Women discussed business next most often, and then health, including weight control. Yes, there are differences between men and women. Big surprise!

But let's not get carried away. The overlap between the sexes on just about any variable is as or more significant than the differences between sexes. So, in the last analysis, we need to treat people as individuals. Understanding group differences can be helpful, but it really doesn't help understand a specific individual.

And I will tell you from my personal experience that when it comes to leadership matters, gender differences are highly overrated. The stereotypes just don't fit when it comes to leadership. The typical stereotype has the male as fact-based, trying to deal with things rationally, and wanting to make decisions quickly without a lot of discussion. Supposedly, they have little concern about the feelings of others; they simply want to get the job done, fast.

The stereotype of the female leader is a person who is more interested in relationships than results. Supposedly, she is caring and empathetic—to a fault. She believes that the process is the end game for all deliberations, rather than getting something done.

I've seen literally thousands of people in leadership positions, not only in higher education, but also in the business and not-for-profit sectors. In my opinion, the effective leaders—the ones who truly make a difference—are sensitive to the concerns of others (but not too concerned or too sensitive). They also are concerned with process, but at the same time they are decisive—they focus on results, and they know how to push the agenda when necessary.

In reality, I find few truly successful leaders who represent the extreme profiles. Neither can weather well under the day-to-day pressure. So, understand group differences, and understand the differences between men and women. But remember, finally, that you're dealing with individuals. When it comes to leadership, the tried and true approaches work for both sexes.

Let's hear from Mary Ann Shaw, who will give a woman's view.

WOMEN, WORKPLACE, AND FAMILY | Mary Ann Shaw[21]

Some say with age come understanding, wisdom, and knowledge. We hope that occurs, but it may or may not be true. What I think can be said about living through multiple decades is that one can look back and reflect on how things have changed, especially if those changes have had a major impact on one's own life. I have been part of the profound change in the role of American women in our society over the past forty years.

Significant change will continue to occur in your lifetime and will have a visible effect on the lives of girls and boys, women and men, families and the workplace far into the twenty-first century.

Understanding the change requires some historical perspective, which I will try to share with you in this essay. I will also talk about adjusting to these changes, provide some suggestions for those in top-level positions for making the workplace a more productive and better environment for both women and men, and then offer some final thoughts. This is not a research document of the times but rather my own brief reflections of the changes and adjustments I have observed through the years.

Recalling the Past

For most of American history, women have been in the workplace contributing to the economic well-being of our communities and country in addition to being in the home raising children, organizing the daily routines, and keeping the family going. What has changed over the past forty years is the substantial increase in the number of women entering the workplace, the types of jobs they are performing, and how these changes have affected the workplace.

During the 1700s and 1800s, on the frontier and in rural America, women worked as partners of men to settle homesteads and ensure the success of family farms. As the industrial age advanced, women were employed as low-

21. Mary Ann Shaw has owned and operated a small business, worked as a teacher, a vice-president for a not-for-profit organization, and a university administrator. She has served on the boards of directors of a bank, three hospitals, a health insurance company and nineteen not-for-profit boards of directors and councils, serving as chair of six.

level factory workers, clerical workers, secretaries, cleaners, and other necessary, low-paying jobs. As education and health care emerged, women became teachers and nurses. These were the jobs primarily open to women. A few women did become doctors, lawyers, managers, or university faculty members, but that road was difficult and laden with many obstacles. The persistent women who succeeded in these professions were true pioneers, but the majority of women were excluded from higher-level managerial and professional jobs. Professional schools either did not admit women or imposed a quota on them. As late as the 1950s and early 1960s, the classified section of most newspapers listed jobs for men and women separately. A woman could apply for the job of bank teller, but not the job of bank manager. A man could apply for both. Pregnant women, in particular, were not welcome in the workplace.

A woman's societal role was to take care of her family and organize the household. If she worked outside the home, she was criticized for not staying home with her children. If she worked outside the home, the work was to be subordinate to her primary role. Extended-family members then often cared for youngsters at home. The husband was considered the primary breadwinner and needed the higher-level, higher-paying job. Thus, the woman's choices were limited and advancement opportunities at work were few.

When a man accepted a position as a pastor of a church congregation, a president of a university, a CEO of a major corporation, or a top government leader, it was assumed the wife would dedicate herself to his job by performing supportive activities to enhance the enterprise. At the time, both men and women for the most part considered these wifely duties an honor.

In the community, women worked as volunteers for many causes, but they rarely served on boards of directors of large not-for-profit organizations with multimillion dollar budgets such as the United Way, the YMCA, or the Community Foundation. Leadership roles in important community organizations were reserved for men. Women who founded now famous not-for-profit organizations were the leaders of their time. Boards of directors of private companies consisted of men with few, if any, women.

Before 1960, organized sports programs in schools and communities were formulated mainly for boys, except at all-girls schools. Scholarships for competitive sports in colleges and universities were primarily reserved for men.

Marking the Change

The women's movement, which paralleled the civil rights movement in the 1960s and 1970s, brought these basic assumptions into very public question. The women's movement sparked a revolutionary shift in thinking about a woman's place in our society. Over the next decades, the combination of national discussion and persistent pressure forced opportunities and choices to open for women beyond anything in the past.

Eventually, women began insisting on entering the managerial track in the business world. Women began running for elective government offices rather than just being members of the League of Women Voters whose sole purpose was to clarify issues for voters. More women went on to higher education and graduate school, thus preparing themselves for higher-paying jobs. Universities began hiring more women as faculty members and administrators. More women insisted on being considered for the job of bank manager.

Boards of directors of major not-for-profit organizations began to extend memberships to more women. Soon some women even became "chairmen" of the board—prompting many a discussion about changing the title to "chair" or "chairwoman" when appropriate. The prefix "Ms." came into use, as it did not proclaim one's marital status, as did "Miss" or "Mrs." Some private companies also began to add a few women to their boards.

Changing at a much slower pace were the requirements for wives of public figures and dignitaries. Both pressure from these wives and the movement of women to the top-level positions in university, business, government, and religious positions began lessening expectations of the spouse.

Occurring at the same time was one of the most momentous but least talked about developments in the field of medicine, the birth control pill. This life-changing pill was developed in the early 1960s and signaled personal freedom for women. For the first time in history, women could exercise definite control over the reproductive cycle of their bodies. The pill would enable women to make strategic choices about how they wanted to live their lives— when and if they wanted to have children, and how many. This discovery allowed women to make career-timing choices with certainty rather than being at the mercy of far less dependable birth control methods.

Adjusting to the Change

During the last three decades of the twentieth century, as many thousands of women moved into the workforce, they advanced into some upper-level management opportunities and jobs previously open only to men. As just one example, women could now work for major food and pharmaceutical companies as managers responsible for large regional sales territories requiring extensive travel around the country, lucrative jobs previously reserved for men. Having this type of job, however, required a shift of attitudes.

With more career opportunities available to them, many women began delaying marriage to their late twenties. They delayed even further having children. Those women with children whose jobs required extensive travel and/or late hours could not be at home to take care of their children all the time. The same was true for women elected officials. Fathers would now have to share some of that responsibility on a regular basis. Nannies and day care became part of our everyday lives. Much pressure was placed on women to move to the workforce, while at the same time many psychologists and child-rearing experts criticized women for leaving their children, especially infants. Stay-at-home moms receded into the background of the national discussion.

During the 1970s, some women who aspired to be CEOs, university presidents, and other high-level leaders decided either not to marry or, if they married, not to have children. The road to the top was extremely daunting, and those women knew they needed to work harder than men to be acknowledged and promoted. It would be extraordinarily difficult to have both a family and a CEO position as a woman. If a married woman wanted to "drop out" of the business world for a while to take care of her children, she was not considered executive material. Women were reluctant to drop out for fear they could not reenter the workforce at a high level. Thus was born the "superwoman" syndrome. Woman were expected to do it all without assistance—take excellent care of the family and home and have a high-level, demanding job in an inflexible workplace.

As we move into the twenty-first century and our society is more supportive of the married, high-level executive woman with children, several additional models appear. Some top women executives in their fifties have teenage children. They choose to marry but delay having children until they have established their careers. They also usually marry men amenable to a two-career marriage, either two high-level career partners or the high-level career wife with a husband who is the family switchboard and has a less pressured job. Occasionally, the husband stays at home.

Another model today is the top woman executive in her forties with children who has decided to take some time off from her work to spend some time with her young children. She has amassed enough money to do this comfortably. She remains on boards of directors of major companies and does some freelance consulting to keep her in the loop. At some time in the future, she hopes to return to another top executive position, but no guarantee exists.

Our society has become more aware and accepting of the fact that some family duties and responsibilities need to be shared. The "superwoman" model has mostly gone by the wayside. More men are accepting larger supportive roles in the family. Women at all levels in the workplace are benefiting from employers more willing to take family responsibilities into consideration when determining benefits and work requirements. Today, stay-at-home moms have gained respect in the national discussion. The number of women deciding not to have children has increased.

With more women in the workplace in more demanding jobs, employers also had to shift gears. Even with all these advances for women combined with many men assuming more of the parenting responsibilities, women still do most of the caretaking and household organizing. They remain the major caregivers and switchboards for the family's activities. In today's world, women often take on caregiving for parents who live longer. This means women may need to miss more work, have the workday interrupted by a sick child, or complete work at a different time than the usual nine-to-five day. Employers now must consider and be attuned to the needs of women workers in order to keep good employees and remain competitive in the marketplace.

Women managers have helped employers better understand the need to make the workplace more supportive of families. Public discussion and pressure from citizens and women legislators have also advanced the needs of women and families. Flextime, day care, work-at-home, job sharing, maternity and parental leave, and telecommuting options have become part of our daily vocabulary.

The many changes occurring since 1960 have created expanded opportunities for many women but have also created much stress. Both women and men are becoming more aware of the need to have a balance between work and home life. This need for balance has helped fuel the development of more supportive workplace work/life options over the past decade. The high level of stress experienced by many has also resulted in myriad magazines, books, and radio and TV talk shows addressing the issue. Dealing with the stress of balancing work and home life is the subject of many discussions and articles, including regular columns published in the *Wall Street Journal.* In order to have more control over their lives, many women have started their own companies. The level of stress produced has also motivated some women and men to forgo the extra money and pressure to enjoy their families and each other.

Taking time off or accepting less money, however, is usually the option only of those who can afford to do so. Most working women do it because they need the money to support their families. They cannot afford to stop working even for a short period of time. Some of these women are single moms; some are married and barely making ends meet with both wife and husband working. For these women, supportive work/life benefit policies are a vital necessity. Even with recent changes, lack of structural support for women in the workplace continues to be a major impediment to their advancing to leadership positions.

Improving the Workplace

Some items from the U.S. Census Bureau:

"In 1900 women made up 18.4 percent of the working population. Today (2000), women make up 46.4 percent of the labor force." [22]

"The percentage of women working in 1998 age 25–45 was over 75 percent." [23]

22. Center for Women and Work at the School of Management and Labor Relations, Rutgers, State University of New Jersey. "Women in the Workforce: Facts about Working Women." Information extracted from Bureau of Labor Statistics, Employment and Earnings, "1900–2000," *http://www.cww.rutgers.edu/dataPages/FactSheet1.pdf.*

23. Heathfield, Susan M., "Women and Work: Then, Now, and Predicting the Future for Women in the Workplace," *About Human Resources*, Mar. 26, 2003. Information extracted from

"71.9 percent of women with children younger than 18 are in the workforce (2000)."[24]

"In 2000, 19 percent of women ages 40–44 had no children, up from 10 percent in 1980."[25]

The number of women in the workforce will continue to increase in the twenty-first century. Some of these women will have no children, but most will be mothers. Because we know that women will continue to hold the primary responsibility for children and family matters even with expanding support from men, we also know that inevitably these responsibilities will flow over into the workplace. Women will be more attracted to employers who offer better and more supportive work/life benefits.

One of the interesting developments is that as employers have installed these policies, men have spent more time on family responsibilities. Consequently, men are also benefiting from the policies and taking advantage of them. These policies appear to help both men and women balance work and family life.

To compete for the best workers, employers will constantly need to focus on improving and expanding these policies. Research and informal evidence indicate these policies do motivate employees to be more productive and contribute significantly to a work environment supportive and welcoming of all.

The recent 2002 Work/Life Benefits Survey by Hewitt Associates of almost one thousand major national companies found that "companies realize that offering these benefits helps employees cope with and balance all of the demands on their time."[26] Survey respondents reported:

- 94 percent offered some form of child care assistance

U.S. Department of Labor: Changes in Women's Work Participation, *http://www.humanresources.about.com/library/aa032603a.htm.*

24. Center for Women and Work, "Women in the Workforce."

25. "American Women, 2003," *About Women's History*, Mar. 2003, *http://www.census.gov/Press-Release/www/2001/cb01–170.html* Available online at *http://www.women'shistory.about.com/library/news/dyk/bldyk/2003o.htm*

26. Hewitt Associates, "2002 Work/Life Benefits Survey," Press Release, May 13, 2002, *http://was4.Hewitt.com/hewitt/resource/newsroom/pressrel/2002/05–13–02.htm* (accessed Oct. 4, 2004; no longer available).

- 74 percent offered flexible work options
- 60 percent offered elder care assistance[27]

The survey found that as the recession deepened companies conducted more complete cost-benefit analyses on all of their programs. "[W]ork/life benefits present a great, and often low-cost, way to motivate employees, engender loyalty and enhance productivity." The fact that these benefits continue to grow suggests that employers recognize their impact on the bottom line.[28]

Many examples of helpful work/life programs abound. One hundred companies are identified in the October 2004 issue of *Working Mother* magazine as the best mother-friendly places to work.[29] The employers offered a wide range of work/life options such as child care, resource and referral for child care, sick/emergency child care, dependent care accounts, health-care accounts, flextime, job sharing, working at home, telecommuting, compressed work week, part-time work, maternity and parental leave, periodic paid and unpaid work interruptions for child and elder care, family counseling, workout areas/memberships, educational opportunities, professional development programs, concierge services, and more. Because we should be viewing mothers' needs as family needs, then obviously these companies are also great places for fathers to work.

These companies also have unique programs that do not cost any money but reinforce a company's dedication to being family supportive. For example, the CEO at one company believes that weekends should be spent with the family. Consequently, meetings cannot be scheduled on Friday afternoons for anyone. Friday is the time for all employees to finish their work and clear off their desks, and they don't take work home over the weekend. Another company asks employees on a regular basis what kind of no-cost/low cost innovations would help moms and dads with their family responsibilities.

Although the hundred companies spotlighted are all large companies, many of the options can be tailored to smaller work environments. I suggest scanning the descriptions of benefits these companies offer for ideas for your workplace.

27. Ibid.
28. Ibid.
29. "Working Mother," Oct. 2004, *http://www.workingmother.com/bestlist.html* (accessed Oct. 4, 2004; no longer available).

Even with expansion of benefits and increased flexibility, some companies find it difficult to keep very talented, upwardly mobile women. Many of these women find the corporate culture and lack of leadership training and opportunities too restrictive. "[A]lthough women make up almost 50 percent of management ranks, they hold only 11 percent of corporate jobs with real clout." [30]

Many are leaving corporations to start their own firms and organizations. This is not difficult for women to accomplish. Today everyone has access to extensive amounts of information through technology, and "women currently between the ages of 25 and 35 have more education than men in the same age group." [31] These highly talented women also have good problem-solving skills and are able to use information effectively.

> "Why do companies lose female talent? High-powered women stated four reasons for leaving their jobs to start firms: the need for more flexibility (51 percent), the glass ceiling (29 percent), unhappiness with the work environment (28 percent), and lack of challenge (22 percent), according to a 1998 study conducted by Catalyst, the National Foundation for Women Business Owners, the Committee of 200, and Salomon Smith Barney. [32]

I highly recommend reading the informative article by Charlene Marmer Solomon in the September 2000 issue of *Workforce* magazine. Ms. Solomon describes numerous proactive ways for companies to keep highly talented women (and men).

Some documented effective strategies include a company's self-assessment of the percentage of women in top assignment areas, expanding opportunities for advancement for identified high-potential women, mentoring, counseling, performance feedback, leadership training, and a customized career advancement plan without long-term career damage. [33]

---

30. Solomon, Charlene Marmer, "Cracks in the Glass Ceiling," *Workforce Management*, September 2000, *http://www.findarticles.com/p/articles/mi/mOFXS/is_9_79/ai_65650779/print.*
    31. Ibid.
    32. Ibid.
    33. Ibid.

As the CEO or leader in your workplace, you will need to make the decision to move in the direction of these supportive work/life strategies and policies. Employees will look to you for direction and support. If you are half-hearted about your support, these strategies and policies will not be developed or, if they are developed, will be poorly implemented. Strong direction and support must come from the top.

Closing Thoughts

Even with significant changes in the workplace, challenges for women will continue to exist. Some men and even women voice reluctance to work for a woman. Many women feel excluded from training opportunities and high-level jobs. Often they feel their contributions are ignored. Sometimes they find themselves isolated in workplaces where only a few other women are employed. Many women work for employers where the lack of good work/life benefits makes it difficult to balance work and family needs.

The presence of these challenges should not deter women from continuing to press for more flexibility, better opportunities and more parity. Often, current practices and barriers exist because few have challenged their existence. People tend to become accustomed to the way things are and do not recognize the need for improvement. On the other hand, current practices and barriers often exist because those benefiting from them do not want to give up control or share the opportunities.

Regardless of the reasons, women will find roadblocks to advancement and support. They will find themselves in situations where they will need to continue to push for changes not only for themselves but also for the betterment of society.

Why would employers limit themselves to a small pool of talent from which to choose? Why would employers choose to ignore implementing benefit policies that we know result in more productivity and loyalty among employees? Truly, all our workplaces, families, and individuals will be better served if employers take advantage of the total diverse talent pool available, the vast array of work/life benefit options available, and opportunities to advance women. Our nation cannot afford to overlook or shut out talent in this highly competitive world economy. Our nation cannot afford to overlook the importance of supporting parents—women *and* men—in achieving healthy children and families. I believe women, particularly young women, will continue to push our nation in the right direction. [MARY ANN SHAW]

Wrapping It Up

- Today's leaders must be open-minded and eager to learn about other people.
- Today's leaders must have the skills to work with people from all sorts of backgrounds. They must be able to "do business" with anyone.
- Today's leaders need to be skilled at unearthing institutional barriers that impede the development of people and have the savvy to know how to eliminate or at least ameliorate them.
- Knowing all this doesn't minimize the fact that you cannot generalize from a group to an individual. Remember what you learned in elementary statistics about the normal curve; this is a reminder that differences within a group are probably as great as differences between groups.
- What you have learned might help you be a nicer person in the workplace. But if you aren't interested in being a nice person, just remember that your organization depends upon getting the most from all its members. You jeopardize the organization's well-being when you deny the contributions of any group of people. You don't have to be nice. Be smart! To be able to compete requires us to be innovative and highly productive, with everyone working for a common cause and exploiting the talents of all those who have the ability and motivation to help.
- In the last analysis, treating all people fairly is the best way to lead. Having a personal philosophy that guides you to fairness will be much to your benefit.

> *Reality Exercise.* Pick a group that you know little about, either through experience or reading, and learn about them. Think about how you can use that knowledge in the workplace and in other groups in which you participate.

7

Organizational Change

Change comes from collaborative effort. All initiatives don't filter up, so the leader must be proactive but sensitive to the need for buy in. It is a combination of top down and bottom up leadership.
— Robert Miron, chairman and CEO of
Advance/Newhouse Communications

In my business, we either adapt to change or disappear. We've adapted successfully by keeping strategies in alignment, growing organically, but also knowing when it is better to acquire the talent we need to keep progressing. Change is a true opportunity to beat the competition.
— Jon Holtz, chairman and CEO,
Win-Holt Equipment Group

Often a new program is just another management fad in an endless series of such fads. A model of change doesn't correspond to reality. This is why so many fail.
— Jeanie Daniel Duck, *Harvard Business Review*,
July/August 2000

Three words come to mind when I think of the [police] Chief: chain of command. If the chief was beside me

while I choked on a gumball, he'd walk to his office and call a deputy chief of support services. The DCSS would inform the major in charge of the criminal investigation section, to alert the captain of the investigative services division. The captain would inform the lieutenant in charge of the crimes against persons unit, and the lieutenant would send a sergeant from homicide to Heimlich my corpse.
> —from Jack Kerley, *The Hundredth Man*

If a leader really wants feedback, he should ask himself whether or not he's created an organization in which there is a place for a fool.
> —Manfred F. R. Kets De Vries, *Harvard Business Review*, January 2004

Corporations, government agencies, and educational institutions spend billions of dollars on trying to change. In business, this expenditure is seen as necessary for survival. In the not-for-profit sector, it's seen as essential to improving the ability to serve clients. One response to the pace of today's change is a revamping of organizational structures. They are becoming flatter, more agile, and team-oriented, thus more empowering.[1]

Our time will be spent less on organizational/structural matters and more on the ways that leaders can effect change in organizations. Others are far more qualified to comment on structural issues than I.

For starters, remember that not all change is good. Abrahamson[2] reminds us that while the change-or-perish mantra is true "in many cases," it also is true that many organizations perish *because* they change. Change can be so disruptive that it tears groups and institutions apart.

This chapter will be an excellent way for you to review the understandings and skills you've already acquired as we apply them in dealing with orga-

---

1. Lussier and Achua, *Leadership.*
2. Eric Abrahamson, "Moving Change," Harvard Business School case study, 2004.

nizational change. For example, the tasks of leaders and various frames used in leadership activities (political, structural, human resources, and symbolic) are important for change agents to know.

The individual skills that we covered—motivating others, resolving conflicts, using the power that is yours, effective decision making, communications, and group effectiveness—all come into play. How nice for you—if you've done your homework well—that you're almost ready to be a change agent. The best way for me to describe how organizations can be structured to effect change is to tell a story. I will tell the Syracuse University story later in this chapter and provide you with take-home ideas and, of course, an assignment or two.

What the Experts Tell Us

First, let's hear what some experts in the field of organizational change tell us about creating the best environment for change.

Set priorities. Nothing new here. Maxwell[3] reminds us that we can't do everything. He suggests using the Pareto Principle, which is the application of a 20–80 ratio to a variety of situations. That is, 20 percent of your priorities will give you 80 percent of your results. So, if you spend your time, energy, money, and personnel on the top 20 percent of your priorities, it'll pay off. He then suggests how you might do this.

Organize your priorities in this way:

1. High importance/high urgency. Tackle these projects first.

2. High importance/low urgency. Set deadlines for completion of these projects, and get them worked into your daily routine, but not immediately.

3. Low importance/high urgency. Find quick, efficient ways to get the work done, or have others do it.

4. Low importance/low urgency. Either take a little time off to do these tasks once in a while or postpone them indefinitely. Maybe they will go away.

The point here: set priorities for yourself, and have those that you interact with do likewise.

Have an effective feedback loop. Sag-Nicole A. Joni[4] offers suggestions for getting good information. She describes the approaches that Clark Clifford used for decades as an advisor to any number of presidents and corporate leaders. Clifford called the insight he provided to such leaders as presidents John F. Kennedy and Lyndon B. Johnson the "third opinion." Clifford said, "Even if he ignores the advice, every president should ensure that he gets a third opinion from selected and seasoned private citizens he trusts." That's a good idea for all of us. And while we should seek opinions from those who work with us, we need to be mindful that people closest to us have their own interests, which don't always coincide with our own or with those of the institution.

Joni offers guidelines for selecting who best can offer us that "third opinion." We have someone we can trust on the personal level, she says, when we can answer yes to these questions: Is he honest and ethical? Will he make good on his word? Is he basically well-intentioned? Will he handle confidential information with care and discretion? Will he be straightforward about what he doesn't know?

3. John Maxwell, *Leadership 101: What Every Leader Needs to Know* (Nashville, Tenn.: Thomas Nelson Publishers, 2002).

4. Sag-Nicole A. Joni, "The Geography of Trust," *Harvard Business Review*, Mar. 2004.

> "People are not your most important asset. The right people are."
> —Jim Collins, *Good to Great*

For picking expert trust, a yes is required for these questions: Is she an expert in her field? Is her knowledge up to date? Does she present credible information to support her positions? Is she able to apply her expertise to our specific situation? Can she offer sage advice on risk, options, and trade-offs?

Earlier in this book, I talked about the importance of getting information from a variety of sources. It clearly is essential in dealing with change efforts. It is also essential to know whom you can trust.

Don't be afraid to copy others. Some of the best ideas come from competing organizations and from groups that are just different from yours. Every change doesn't have to come from a creative spark. Rather, your rule of thumb should be: first examine change initiatives that can be copied, to avoid reinventing the wheel.

Don't forget the importance of people. Jim Collins[5] and his research team identified a set of elite companies that made the leap from good to great results and maintained them for at least fifteen years. He says you need to "get the right people on the bus, the wrong people off the bus, and the right people in the right seats. After that you can figure out where to drive it." Obviously he believes that the right people are more important to organizational effectiveness than the right vision. In other words, to Collins, the right people help to create that vision.

Use technology wisely. Collins believes that good to great companies think differently about the role of technology. They never use it as the primary means of igniting change; they only use it strategically—as a tool to get to the next level.

Patience is extremely important. John Kotter[6] believes that real change often takes years. It requires at least eight steps: (1) establishing a sense of urgency, (2) forming a powerful guiding coalition, (3) creating a vision, (4) com-

5. Jim Collins, *Good to Great: Why Some Companies Make the Leap and Others Don't* (New York: Harper Business, 2001).

6. Kotter, *Leading Change*.

municating the vision, (5) empowering others to act on the vision, (6) planning for and creating short-term wins, (7) consolidating improvements and producing still more change, and (8) institutionalizing new approaches.

Change, to Kotter and others, is not a passing fad but rather something that is substantial and that becomes a part of an organization's culture. It takes time, patience, and good use of the understanding and skills you have already acquired.

The Syracuse University Experience

Now I want to tell you a story that deals with organizational change. Many of the principles that you've already learned in this book, and in this chapter, apply. For the most part, I learned them through experience. Here's the story and the take-home value.[7]

Like many good, selective, private institutions of higher education in the late 1980s, Syracuse University was hit with the double whammy of a demographic downturn in the numbers of college-bound students and a time of great economic uncertainty.

We had some difficult decisions to make. Would we try to compete for a greater share of the decreasing cohort of eighteen-year-olds projected through the 1990s? Or would we enroll fewer students, and thus ensure that we would keep quality high?

We chose to allow undergraduate enrollments to fall by more than 2,500 students. Naturally, there had to be a corresponding decrease in the numbers of faculty and staff.

By 1999, we cut in excess of $60 million from our base budget and became smaller not only in our student body, but also by 165 faculty members and 400 staff. We did this without disenfranchising the tenured faculty or gutting our complement of outstanding tenure-track young faculty. But that's another story for another time.

The process began in 1992 with a $60 million cut, phased in over five years, followed by another $6 million cut, which we euphemistically referred to as fine-tuning.

Also, we created a new vision: to become the nation's leading student-

7. Kenneth A. Shaw, adapted from a speech given at the University of Kansas, Oct. 2004.

centered research university. We decided that this was an opportunity for renewal and transformation, understanding that cutting budgets alone would not serve to make us better.

We made the cuts strategically rather than across the board. For example, the academic side absorbed a 17 percent cut, while the administrative side was cut 22 percent. And within each academic area, priorities were set and followed so that some programs received budget add-ons while others were cut. One program had its operating funding cut more than 30 percent.

But we didn't stop with budget cuts. Rather, we used this process as an opportunity to become a better place—an opportunity for both renewal and transformation. That transformation will never be complete—we've created a new set of problems that subsequent chancellors will have to handle, but the momentum we've started will not stop.

At the time our restructuring program was announced in 1992, we launched thirty-three initiatives for improvement. Three or four of them didn't work out, but most did, including an improved faculty reward system, the integration of undergraduate research and teaching, the improvement of advising, a much stronger first-year experience, the promotion of active learning, the blending of liberal arts and professional studies, improvements in retention, better services through a quality improvement program, and any number of unanticipated but welcomed spin-offs that occurred in the spirit of the student-centered research university enterprise.

The accomplishments after thirteen years—from 1991 to 2004—made me very proud. We achieved:

- A more diverse faculty

- In excess of a 90 percent increase in high school students coming from the top 10 percent of their class

- A two-thirds increase in our two-year retention rate and an improvement in our graduation rate from around 70 percent of entering freshman to over 81 percent.

- Greater alumni support of our successful Commitment to Learning fund drive, to the tune of over $370 million, and over $700 million during my term of office.

- Numerous higher education recognitions, including the Hesburgh Award for Innovation in Faculty Development.

• A much better university. *Change* magazine said: "Today Syracuse is down the road toward its becoming the nation's leading student-centered research university; it can serve as a model for institutional change and leadership in the cause of undergraduate educational reform."

So there has been a transformation—not everything worked, more remains to be done—but we learned a lot, which I will pass on to you now in your take-home tips.

Having a crisis really helps. Ours was not quite a crisis, but it was a serious challenge. Had we done nothing, we would have found ourselves with a crisis—serious financial difficulties and no plan to work our way through them. We knew we had to do something because 85 percent of our operating budget came from tuition and auxiliary services that serve our students. We had to cut our budget, and we had to be a student-centered place in more than just rhetoric.

Perhaps your organization doesn't have that kind of challenge or crisis. This is for you to decide: Do you have a crisis or a real challenge? Or do you have just a small problem that you believe will go away? If you feel you've got a small problem that'll go away, remember, not all small problems go away.

Transparency is essential. At Syracuse, we opened our books to everyone, something unique for a private institution. In fact, the news spread nationally when the *New York Times* described our financial difficulties. It didn't hurt our enrollment, although many felt it would.

The materials we released showed how and where we spent our money, which schools and colleges were bringing in more money than they spent, and which weren't doing well. And some truly weren't doing well. At that time, a good dean was expected to stay within budget; there was little consideration of matching income brought in (after overhead is paid) with expenses.

All of this openness gave us the credibility to move forward. Some mistakenly thought we had billions of dollars in reserve and hence no problem. Showing our reserves solved that problem. Some thought we were broke and headed for financial bankruptcy. Showing our reserves helped people understand that bankruptcy was far from the case—that, in fact, we were poised to spend money to save money if it made sense. (We did and it did.)

It is essential to focus on an institution's mission, vision, and core values.

Change doesn't come out of nowhere; it has to be grounded in what the institution represents. At Syracuse, we used our values, mission, and a new vision statement to direct our energies. We repeatedly stressed core values—quality, caring, diversity, innovation, and service—during the first few years of restructuring. Our mission statement was revised to state that together we could promote learning through teaching, research, scholarship, creative accomplishment, and service. That, too, was frequently repeated. And we crafted a new vision for the future—to be the nation's leading student-centered research university. These three things—our values, mission, and vision—had to and did guide our efforts.

Regardless of an institution's situation, services to the students and the learning community can always be improved. This can usually be done quickly. We did it through a quality improvement program that involved every staff member. It proved to be far more complex than necessary, but at the end of the day services improved greatly. What we learned was the need to focus on our "customer." This means we needed to ask ourselves who our customer was, and then ask what their needs were and how best to meet them. The biggest gain from this enterprise was getting groups from all over the campus to work together through the training process. I won't say it took hold 100 percent, but it did work, and it greatly improved morale.

Institutions must walk the talk. As we were cutting budgets, we spent $2 million over three years to improve teaching. We gave priority to faculty projects that enhanced teaching at the lower division level. That commitment was carried through to fund a variety of such projects through the University Vision Fund administered by the vice chancellor and provost.

In the early 1990s, we received a major gift of about $5 million. While that money could have been used in a variety of ways, it went to the development of the Meredith Professorships. These are singular honors for professors whose excellence as teachers sets them apart. Two are appointed each year and serve a three-year term. They are provided $22,000 as a salary add-on for those three years plus $10,000 in funds for professional development for them and their departments. The goal is to enable them to share their teaching expertise with their fellow faculty members. The Meredith program has been expanded to honor up-and-coming young scholar-teachers.

Don't be afraid to borrow from others. Remember the goal is innovation, not invention. It's okay to borrow good ideas from your peers; actually it's okay to borrow from those below you in the pecking order. Some very great ideas come from institutions that you don't feel are as distinguished as yours. Focus on the strength of the ideas and how they can be adapted, rather than on who's doing it.

Keep the pressure on. Complacency is always tempting. I like to describe Syracuse as a place that's dissatisfied. We've done a lot, but we know we must do more. We also know we don't have the resources to do all the things we would like to do. Hence, the healthy dissatisfaction — it requires us to make the most of what we have and never to be satisfied.

To enhance our academic enterprise, our board allowed us to take $5 million a year from our endowment over ten years for academic improvements. You won't be surprised to hear that each year this money wasn't given out across the board. Under the leadership of our provost, an academic plan was developed that focused on four areas of emphasis: Information Management and Technology, Environmental Systems and Quality, Collaborative Design, and Citizenship and Social Transformation — all interdisciplinary programs requiring high levels of collaboration and cooperation. The plan also calls for continuing improvements in the undergraduate learning environment.

This money could have been used for a lot of things, but we focused it on our aspirations. You have to keep the pressure on and you do so by walking the talk.

Give people the tools to change. Too often, we misinterpret resistance to change as coming from people who are opposed to everything. In fact, people can deal with even enormous change if you put their fears aside and give them the reason and the tools to change. We confronted people's fears by reminding them that once the cuts were made, if we committed 100 percent to our vision, things would get much better. And they did. And while cutting budgets, we spent millions of dollars on curricular reform, quality improvement programs, and the beefing up of our in-house training programs for staff. We defined ourselves as a learning community in which all were expected to learn. People did buy into the program, and we continued to provide resources for faculty and staff to continue to learn.

Don't forget triage in dealing with resistance to change. In an earlier chapter, I mentioned that there are three types of people when it comes to change:

those who would support the change if it can be demonstrated that it's to their and their organizations' benefit; fence-sitters waiting to decide if the change is going to take; and determined resisters of change, regardless of what is proposed. Remember, spend most of your time shoring up the committed and encouraging the fence-sitters. Trying to woo the strongly opposed diverts your energies and raises questions about your true commitment from those who will support you if things are handled right. Although we didn't have too many people in the third category, we didn't give them much of our time either.

Don't devalue the role of persistence. In my observations and study of leadership, I've noticed that very little attention is given to persistence. We read and hear much about charisma, transforming leaders, the personal characteristics of leaders, and the environmental influences that affect what leaders can and cannot do, but little is said about what I believe is highly underrated—the importance of persistence.

I've seen effective leaders with dandruff on their suits and halting speech who somehow remain standing and persist in getting their programs across. Similarly, institutional change requires more than just the persistence of a chancellor or provost. It requires people believing in improving the learning environment. It requires people willing to not give up, to persist. Many of you reading this don't work at an institution of higher education. The take-home points you learned in the story can be adapted to any number of situations. Give it some thought.

> *Reality Exercise.* Think about an organization, business, service group, or club to which you belong. What changes, if any, do you feel are needed? What understandings and techniques that you've learned could you use to be an agent of change?

Dealing with Organizational Grief

Sometimes the need for change is so great that no matter how skilled the leader, no matter how dedicated the group members, it will be seriously traumatic. Good examples would be a corporate takeover, competition-driven changes in salary and fringe benefits, large staff cutbacks, or the elimination of an entire unit.

That's when organizations go through a grieving process similar to what an individual feels when confronting his own or a loved one's death. Elisabeth Kübler-Ross[8] and others have defined the stages of grief.

Denial. Refusing to deal with the situation's reality often becomes a necessary buffer. It gives us time to absorb the truth and avoid overreacting to bad news. It also can lead to the next line of defense in combating sadness and vulnerability.

Anger. The defiance and righteous indignation that attend bad news are normal, though often difficult for those in leadership positions to accept. As long as these feelings don't become destructive, they should be respected in the short term. Of course, it's important not to get stuck in this space, since anger can become a very destructive force.

Bargaining. As members of the organization attempt to postpone the inevitable, they promise to be "good." They'll work longer hours, brainstorm solutions, conduct a bake sale—whatever it takes, if only the bad news will go away. Bargaining is denial with an agenda.

Depression. People give up in their attempts to push the truth away. It's a very difficult time. And it's a step in the preparation for accepting loss because loss is, after all, a very painful thing. Sadness and gloom are natural reactions—but like the previous stages, they can't last forever.

Acceptance. At first accepting loss seems to be the absence of feeling, but as time progresses acceptance becomes hope as renewal leads the way to growth and positive change.

The process of grieving is rarely entirely linear. Some steps are skipped, to be revisited later. Others can dominate for longer periods of time. But it is important for leaders to understand that this happens. They shouldn't take anger personally nor be overly critical of the denial or institutional funk that sets in. In a previous publication,[9] I suggested strategies for dealing with organizational grief. Here they are again.

---

8. Elisabeth Kübler-Ross, *On Death and Dying* (New York: Macmillan, 1969).

9. Kenneth A. Shaw, *The Successful President: "Buzzwords" on Leadership* (Phoenix, Ariz.: Oryx Press, 1999).

What Does Terry Say about Change?

Terry, in your experience, what are the most important things to know about effecting change?

1. You need strong estimating skills—that is, you need to be able, through data and experience, to determine if the change is going to be worth it.

2. While a long-term vision is important, you need short-term goals that can be realized.

3. You need a change agent—a leader who is behind the project "come hell or high water." This person removes obstructions—so that momentum is maintained.

Terry, when change efforts fail, what is usually the cause?

1. Having a thousand ideas, but no focus or follow-through.

2. Not rewarding those responsible for implementing change.

3. Leaders who show ambivalence—they are not behind the project "come hell or high water."

Leadership Strategies for Organizational Grief

Leaders benefit in three important ways when they accept grieving as a normal process, First, they can help others understand what is going on and therefore move toward acceptance more rapidly. Second, they can deal with the anger directed toward them without taking it personally. And third, they can give due attention to the emotional aspects of change, instead of retreating to the safety of strictly rational approaches.

Here are some effective techniques for dealing with the stages of organizational grief.

Repetition. It's estimated that people need to hear a message twenty-eight times before they internalize it. Meet denial by gently but firmly repeating and reinforcing the truth. Make use of meetings, publications, public events, and other communication outlets as opportunities to outline the situation and restate the reasons for hope. Be certain that key members of the organization have the information and support they need to serve as spokespersons as well. Enlist the assistance of leaders of other organizations and consultants who have the luxury of illuminating the truth and then escaping before denial turns to anger.

Personal Detachment. When the anger surfaces, detach from it even as you accept it. Concentrate on the reality and the hope for the future; avoid entirely returning the anger with your own. At the same time, stay close to the organization and its members. It may be very tempting to head to higher ground during periods of great stress, but a leader's visibility is critically important at these times.

Optimism. Organization-wide depression is best countered with solidly grounded optimism. When members express the belief that things will never get any better, the leader's job is to convince them that they're wrong. While words of encouragement are very helpful, actions are even better. This might be a great time to reward people publicly for outstanding work, introduce a family-friendly program like flextime, or host an all-staff party. The point is to keep things moving by involving people fully in the process of renewal.

Timing. Stay close to the organization so you can act immediately when acceptance becomes widespread—at no time will the organization be more receptive to progress. People have stopped hoping for the good old days to return. Now they're ready to take hold of the vision for the future.

Reality Exercise. Think of situations in which you've seen institutions and organizations go through the grieving stages of change. To what extent did the model I provided explain how things happened? What was different? What would you do to move a group to acceptance?

8

It's Back to You

The leader's first task is to be the trumpet that sounds a clear sound.

—Peter Drucker, *The Effective Executive*

Be ashamed to die until you have won a victory for humanity.

—Horace Mann

Don't confuse fame with success. Madonna is one, Helen Keller is the other.

—Irma Bombeck

Some day, I hope you get the chance to live like you were dying.

—Tim McGraw song written by
Craig Wiseman and Tim Nichols

When we started our journey, I told you that we would end up full-circle—back to you. In this chapter, I will discuss some personal issues that needed to be a part of your being an intentional leader. They are ethical principles, living a balanced life, and your responsibility for the leadership development of others. Let's start with ethics.

The Ethical You

Make no mistake about it—ethical leaders are good leaders. You will remember in our section on cross-cultural issues that the most sought after and admired leaders around the world were honest, forward-looking, confident, and inspiring. In most international surveys conducted over the past thirty years, honesty is valued first. Why? Kouzes and Posner[1] say, "because we don't want to be lied to, we want to be told the truth. We want a leader who knows right from wrong. . . . When we follow someone we believe to be dishonest, we come to realize that we've compromised our own integrity. In time, we not only lose respect for the leader, we lose respect for ourselves."

1. James M. Kouzes and Barry Z. Posner, *The Leadership Challenge*, 3d ed. (San Francisco: Jossey-Bass, 2002).

"My father started this business. His creed was brief but absolute, and it is followed today. 'Always be kind. Always be true.'"
—William E. Allyn, past chairman and CEO, Welch Allyn, Inc.

Seidman[2] puts it another way. "When do we trust someone? Only when we have experience that provides tangible evidence that someone is not taking advantage of us—that they can be relied on to be true to their words; then we will consider them trustworthy." Seidman believes the only way to conduct your affairs is to proceed as if you have nothing to hide. "But, before you behave as if you have nothing to hide, you really better have nothing to hide."

And ethical behavior makes good economic sense. Reichheld and Teal[3] studied the economic value of business loyalty. They found that product loyalty or loyalty to a firm helps to generate superior results. Loyalty comes from the personal integrity of the senior leadership team and its ability to put its principles into practice. They feel that this is also true for Web-based companies. "Price does not rule the Web; trust does."

So, with all of the apparent good reasons for ethical behavior, why the recent corruption scandals at formerly respected organizations such as Enron, WorldCom, Tyco, Health South, and others? Why don't we always behave ethically? I will try to address these questions in this section. Also, I will define what I mean by ethics and ethical behavior, show some examples of ethical

"Our code is simple: Set the standard. Treat everyone with respect, regardless of position. If you make a mistake, admit it. And give credit to others."
—John Couri, cofounder of Duty-Free International.

2. Dov Seidman, "The Case for Ethical Leadership," *The Academy of Management Journal* 18, no. 2 (May 2004): 134.

3. Frederick Reichheld and Thomas Teal, *The Loyalty Effect: How Today's Leaders Build Lasting Relationships* (Boston: Harvard Business School Press, 2000).

> "Never ask someone to do something that you wouldn't do."
> —Dan Mezzalingua, former chairman and
> CEO of Production Products Co.

principles, and attempt to put this all together in a way that will be helpful to you in charting your ethical course.

Let's begin with a definition. This won't be a dictionary or ethics textbook definition but a more simplified one that I hope will keep us on track. It works for me; it can work for you.

Ethics Defined

Ethics are both beliefs (standards, rules of behavior) and behavior itself. Our beliefs are a set of basic working tenets for our interactions with people and institutions.

How we apply these ethical beliefs is our ethical behavior. So, the extent to which the two, beliefs and behavior, are in alignment makes for our being happier people and having the potential for leadership. When these two are not in alignment, we rationalize our behavior through a number of devices I'll refer to later, or we feel extreme guilt. In any event, it is most difficult for leaders to maintain their strength if their behavior is not ethical.

Discussion of ethics has been around for centuries. Twenty-five hundred years ago, Confucius had thoughts that still apply today:

"Hold fast to what is good and the people will be good."

"The virtue of the good man is as the wind and that of the bad man as the grass. When the wind blows, the grass will bend."

"Let the leader show rectitude in his personal character and things will go well, even without directions from him."

Being ethical, of course, means that you're a person of good character. Komives et al.[4] define a person of character as someone who is:

- trustworthy (is honest, has integrity, keeps promises, is loyal)

4. Komives, Lucas, and McMahon, *Exploring Leadership.*

What Does Terry Say?

In business, if you take the long-term view, you will always behave ethically. In our company, once we have reached an agreement over a work product with a client, we will finish on time and, if anything, go beyond our commitment. This is the right thing to do, but it is also good for business. We want future business with any company we deal with, and this is the way to ensure it.

- respectful (is courteous, nonviolent, nonprejudiced, accepting)
- responsible (is accountable, pursues excellence, shows self-restraint)
- fair (just, equitable, open, reasonable, unbiased)
- caring (kind, compassionate, empathetic, unselfish)
- a good citizen (is law-abiding, does his/her share, performs community service, protects the environment)

Some professions, such as law, medicine, and counseling, have their own codes of ethics that guide the behavior of its members. It is helpful to know others' views on ethics. It helps guide our thoughts; but in the last analysis leaders must develop their own ethical map to guide them. We'll get to that later.

Let's deal with why individuals and institutions suffer ethical lapses. First, individuals. Some of us don't have an ethical code to guide us. Anything goes to achieve the objective. There are people in business and in life who, while accepting the trappings of society, that is, good schools for their children, making a good living, having prestige, etc., deny the acceptable means of getting there. In the long pull, they, too, will lose ground as people and certainly as leaders.

More common, however, is that we have our set of ethical principles, but for a variety of reasons we choose to violate them. And when we do, we rationalize our behavior in numerous ways. Anand, et al.[5] say that one of the most in-

5. Vikus Anand, Blake Ashford, and Makendra Joshi, "Business as Usual: The Acceptance and Perpetuation of Corruption in Organizations," *The Academy of Management Journal* 18, no. 2 (May 2004).

triguing findings in white-collar crime literature is that corrupt individuals tend not to believe themselves to be corrupt. They use a variety of rationalizing tactics to allow themselves to look at their ethical lapses in a way that makes them acceptable to themselves and others. Here are some of these rationalizations:

Denial of responsibility. "What can I do? My arm is being twisted"; "It is none of my business what the corporation does in overseas bribery."

Denial of injury. "No one was really harmed"; "It could have been worse."

Denial of victim. "They deserved it"; "They chose to participate."

Social waiving. "Others are worse than we are."

Appeal to higher loyalties. "We answer to a more important cause"; "I would not report it because of my loyalty to my boss."

Metaphor of the ledger. "We earned the right." We rationalize our behavior by believing that we are entitled because of our accrued credits (time and effort) in our jobs or other activities. So, as individuals we stray and find ways to justify it.

Patrick Kushe is a businessman who strayed from his ethical tenets. For it, he spent four years in federal and foreign prisons. He is now a consultant in business ethics. He cites eight critical-thinking errors common in most unethical behavior. I want to focus on entitlement, which is one of the eight.

Kushe was a very successful businessman in real estate and lived in a nice neighborhood in a nice house. He had a wonderful family, country club membership — just about anything one would want. But as he looked around, he noticed many had it better. It began to gnaw at him. "I work harder than these people and I'm smarter. I have a right to have all the things they have. I am entitled." This took Kushe down a slippery slope he's still trying to reclimb. Feeling entitled to much more than the basic necessities is dangerous

"Trustworthiness is the foundation of trust. Trust is the emotional bank account between two people that enables them to have a win-win agreement. Trust, or the lack of it, is at the root of success or failure in relationships and in the bottom line results of business, industry, education, and government."
— Steven R. Covey, *Principle-Centered Leadership*

"The biggest ethical pitfalls are: (1) A reluctance to speak up against fraud and waste and a corporate culture that encourages silence, and (2) A reluctance to admit when we are wrong. This is where we dig the deepest hole and things just get worse."
—Michael Dritz, chairman, Dritz Enterprises LLC, New York

thinking. One wise person once told me that I might not like it if I get what I deserve.

In short, as individuals we often stray, either because we have no ethical code ourselves or because we are tempted by feelings of entitlement or greed.

Many ethical lapses are a result of the social environment of our institution. In business situations it's harder to say no to a boss who demands making the numbers work out, or to go over the head of a boss who is doing something unethical. And we are reluctant to report others for fear of retaliation, either from management or from coworkers. The social context, then, often creates dissonance between our own values and the actions we feel we must take to confirm to group norms.

Ethical Principles and Behavior Are Not Easy

Klebe Trevino and Brown[6] recently described five business myths dealing with ethics. They bear repeating at this time.

Myth 1: It's easy to be ethical. Not so, say the authors. Often various ethical approaches conflict with one another, leaving the decision maker with little clear guidance. Examples are multinational businesses with manufacturing facilities in developing countries struggling to deal with employment practice issues. Most Americans believe employing children is harmful and contrary to their beliefs. But children routinely contribute to family income in many cultures. If corporations simply refuse to hire them, or fire them because they are too young, they may resort to begging or even more dangerous

6. Linda Klebe Trevino and Michael Brown, "Managing to Be Ethical: Debunking Five Business Ethics Myths," *The Academy of Management Journal* 18, no. 2 (May 2004).

employment, such as prostitution. What action produces the greater harm? Not as easy as it sounds.

They believe also, as I've said earlier, that some individuals don't know when they're in ethical dilemmas; that is, they don't have a set of standards themselves. We're daily faced with these dilemmas—conflicts over our various ethical priorities or ways of looking at things

Myth 2: Unethical behavior in business is simply the result of bad apples. Wrong, Klebe Trevino and Brown say. They show just how influential group pressure is on individuals. They refer to a fifty-foot-long pile of stolen items taken by teenagers in New Britain, Connecticut, during a scavenger hunt. These normally law-abiding girls stole these items in a single evening but didn't believe they had done anything wrong. They describe another incident near Chicago where high school girls engaged in an aggressive and brutal hazing ritual that landed five young women in the hospital. These are not bad people, they say; the examples simply show the influence of peers to be very, very powerful.

Klebe Trevino and Brown conclude that "most people . . . are followers when it comes to ethics. When asked or told to do something unethical, most will do so. This means that they must be led toward ethical behavior or be left to flounder."

Myth 3: Ethics can be managed through formal ethics codes and programs. The authors do believe that codes and having a formal program are important. But more important is whether the organization is walking the talk: Do the actions of leaders, and the informal messages they send, coincide with the code?

They describe the fall of the giant accounting firm Arthur Anderson, in

> "Hubris and greed grow as the stock market goes up because some people in a position to do so start comparing themselves and their wealth to others and say to themselves they are better and therefore deserve more, which will give them greater recognition and leads to even greater hubris."
>
> —Arthur Rock, principal, Arthur Rock and Co.

> "It's not that humans have become any more greedy than in genera-
> tions past. It is that the avenues to express greed [have] grown so
> enormously."
>
> —Alan Greenspan

spite of decades of attention to ethics beginning with the founder, who believed that "the day Arthur Anderson loses the public trust is the day we are out
of business." They strayed; their frequently told stories to reinforce the importance of ethics wasn't enough.

Myth 4: Ethical leadership is mostly about leader integrity. Wrong again,
they say. Being perceived as a moral person is not enough in leadership.
"Being a moral person only tells followers what the leaders will do. It doesn't
tell them what the leader expects them to do." A moral leader, then, leads not
only by example but also by setting standards for others to follow.

Myth 5: People today are less ethical than they used to be. Again, no, according to the authors. Unethical behavior is nothing new. From student
cheating to corporate ethical lapses, cheating hasn't increased that much,
they believe. New technologies and learning approaches create greater opportunities for cheating. But the problem isn't that more people flout the law.

Let's Make It a Bit More Complex

Have I made things unnecessarily complex? Let me muddy the waters a bit
more before I give you a set of principles to help put things together. Veiga et
al.[7] explain why corporate managers bend the rules. From polling performed
with the Academy of Management's Executive Advisory Panel, they estimate
that about 70 percent of all executives sometimes do so. Their reward? They
come off looking effective.

The authors cite three major reasons for rule bending:

Performance-based judgment calls. They modify the rules to get the job
done or to avoid hurting the organization and its people.

7. John F. Veiga, Timothy D. Golden, and Kalp Leen Deschart, *The Academy of Management Journal* 18, no. 2 (May 2004).

Perception that the rules are faulty. They're believed to be ambiguous, out of date, or too inflexible to deal with the situation.

The presence of norms that permit such violations. Unspoken norms often are stronger than company policy.

We can't simply say that people who bend the rules are bad. If it were that easy, life itself would be easy. Rather, many of these individual judgments result in more moral decisions and improved effectiveness, says Veiga et al. Consider the case of a middle manager whose employee worked day and night, all weekend, on an emergency. The company's policy permits no overtime and no compensatory time off. The manager, nevertheless, tells the employee to take off two days of his own choosing and to mark them down as sick days. This was clearly against the rules. You decide whether it was the right or wrong thing to do.

So, having high ethical principles and adhering to them is a good thing. However, it isn't always easy, and the issues are often extremely complex. Where does this leave us? Let me suggest a set of principles to guide you.

1. You need to have your own code of ethics. It should be something that you live by in your personal and professional lives. It should provide the basis for unavoidable decisions.

2. In the workplace, and in other institutions in which you're involved, be certain that you understand the existing ethical culture. Attempt to know both what is stated and what is practiced.

3. Look for congruence and inconsistency. The greater the congruence between your ethical standards and the code that your business or organization lives by, the happier you'll be. That isn't always your choice. Sometimes the discrepancy is so great you have to leave the group. However, you might stay and seek change, moving the organization to what you believe is a higher standard. That may not be possible for economic or other reasons. You might find yourselves having to make a conscious decision to go along, even if it's something that doesn't fit your code. I'm not making a value judgment as to what you should do; these are very personal and difficult decisions. I am saying that you should confront them consciously rather than try to rationalize your way through them.

4. Be cognizant of which parts of your code sometimes compete with one another. Know that you'll have to make choices and find yourself, at different

"When you clarify the principles that will govern your life, and the ends that you seek, you give purpose to your daily decisions. A personal creed gives you a point of reference for navigating the sometimes stormy seas of organizational life."

—James M. Kouzes and Barry Z. Posner,
The Leadership Challenge

times, weighing various aspects of your code. Say family involvement and successfully completing a work plan are both extremely important to you. Everything is okay until they actually conflict, forcing you to make a choice. Perhaps your child has the lead role in the school play, and you are under pressure to complete that work plan. Then you must choose between missing a very important family event and finishing your project. What do you do? We all make these choices. Looking back, I was much happier when my choices came down on the side of my family. But that's my value judgment. The important thing is that you know you are making these choices and that competing interests make for less than a perfect situation.

5. If you are in a leadership position, communicate your organization's ethical standards and ensure that ethical issues are discussed. Create a system that people believe results in the good guys getting ahead and the bad guys losing out. This also means creating safety valves that permit and encourage exposure of less-than-ethical practices.

6. Be kind to yourself. If you have a code and try to live by it, know you won't be perfect. Do the best you can but confront openly, at least to yourself, the conflicts you have. But be prepared to move on after you've made a decision, even when it turns out to be bad. These dilemmas are a part of being human, and none of us is perfect.

7. Remember, your ethical behavior determines your ability to lead. Living by your own and your organization's codes is a must if you are to lead.

I said it wasn't easy. Don't allow yourself the luxury of ignoring a part of your humanness.

Let's hear from Joseph O. Lampe, former chairman of Lampe and Company, a real estate development and management firm in Phoenix, Arizona.

My first boss [in 1955] always reminded me that you can't make a good deal with a bad person. The thrust was that in all of your dealings, play it above board with everyone. If you get the reputation for being unethical, the vast majority of persons you deal with will probably walk away from working with you. The reality is, your reputation does precede you!

A good rule is to treat others as you wish to be treated. The old adage, "Do unto others as you would have them do unto you," is as true now as it was hundreds of years ago. Here is the best advice I can give you.

1. Remember what you say today may come back to haunt you.

2. Don't be greedy. Greed has caused too many business people to feed their greed with unethical actions.

3. Let other people retain their dignity. A prime example: Allow people the option to resign if you are terminating them.

4. Take advice from competent, honest professionals. Don't find someone who will, for a price, tell you what you want to hear. Don't ask them how you can get around regulations.

5. Don't fool yourself. If you "fudge" and say, "It's just for this one time," I guarantee it will just be the start. The more you get away with misrepresentations, the more likely you are to do it again and again.

6. Don't think you are above having your unethical practices come home to haunt you. It's a long climb to the top but a short fall to the bottom.

Reality Exercise. It is important that you begin, today, to think about your own ethical code, knowing that whatever rules you establish are guideposts, not absolutes. A personal code allows you to make judgments and to behave in a way that for you is most ethical. To help you in this path, I am taking the risk of indicating my personal code. I do so knowing that it is incomplete and could stand much improvement. I want you to do the same and to see that it's okay to not have a perfectly stated code.

My code:

1. My family is the most important thing in my life. I want to do what I can to see them grow and prosper and to have good relationships with them. When making difficult decisions, I will try to ensure that the decision I make is best for those I love the most.

2. I will treat others with respect, acknowledging their uniqueness as people and their desire to be heard.

3. I will not lie to people. My word is important. I will not, however, use my truthfulness as a crutch for cruelty.

4. I will be reliable in my dealings with people. This is more that being truthful—it involves people knowing that if I say I will do something, they can count on my doing it.

5. Work is important to me. I want to work hard, and I want to believe that the work I am doing makes things better for people. I am willing to work very hard to see that happen.

6. In my work, I also want to see my colleagues grow. I have a responsibility for creating and sustaining an environment that helps people reach their potential.

7. In the work setting, I need to set a good example—one that is consistent with my own values and that of the institution I serve.

8. It is important for me to believe that my time on earth results in the betterment of others. Perhaps this will be in small ways, but I want to believe that my time here, whether it is in work, family, or other activities, does, by my example and the results of my efforts, make things better for others.

9. I try to involve myself in activities in which my own ethical standards and that of the institution I'm serving are congruent. When conflicts between the two occur, it is very difficult for me.

10. Sometimes my own values and the values of the institution I am serving are competing. I acknowledge these times and work through them the best I can.

11. I know that I am not perfect, that my own values are incomplete. I also know that sometimes I stray from them. Sometimes in weighing competing values, I make the wrong decision. I know, however, that I can only try to do what is right. Knowing I'm not perfect makes me human.

Self-Awareness Exercise. Develop your own ethical principles that will guide your behavior. Write them down in a way that's meaningful for you. This is not to please others, although I hope that you'll be willing to share it with others. Do it in a way that's a constant re-minder for you and is easy for you to follow.

And we move on from there. As you deal with ethical issues, you'll no doubt want to keep your own code close at hand, and refer to it frequently. You will also need to evaluate your actions vis-à-vis the code, to learn from your experience.

You're not perfect, either. But you are human—very, very human, and that makes you great.

Living a Balanced Life

What disturbs people's minds is not events, but their judgment of events.
—Albert Glaser, *Stations of the Mind*

I regard every defeat as an opportunity.
—Jean Merret

Attitude is the mother of luck.
—Pat Riley, *The Winner Within*

Only a mediocre person is always at his best.
—Somerset Maugham

If a thing is worth doing, it is worth doing badly.
—Lord Chesterton

It seems we've come full circle. I started our journey by helping you learn more about yourself—your strengths and your weaknesses—emphasizing the importance of self-awareness. We then moved on to the development of skills for being more effective with people in one-to-one, group, and institutional settings. From there, you've developed an understanding of the importance of culture and a variety of other issues to guide you to becoming an effective leader. Now we come back to you. We started the previous section with the

ethical you. You were asked to develop an ethical code. You will find that code helpful as you read this section on the balanced you.

For you to lead intentionally, you need to be healthy. If you're stressed, unbalanced, always exhausted, or overwhelmed, you're not likely to be effective. And you'll become less effective each day.

A balanced life will greatly help you to overcome these personal dilemmas. Yet, achieving perfect balance is impossible—there's no such thing. One woman executive was heard to say, "I can't be a perfect mom and executive each day. Something has to give."

Lee and King [8] correctly remind us that balance doesn't mean equal time for work and leisure. It means weighing the importance of different activities

8. Robert J. Lee and Sara N. King, *Discovering the Leader in You: A Guide to Realizing Your Personal Leadership Potential* (San Francisco: Center for Creative Leadership and Jossey-Bass, 2001).

at different points in your life. Your solution to the balance problem will be different from someone else's. And your solutions will change depending upon where you are in the age cycle. For example, in my early professional years, with three young children, balance to me was going full-tilt at my work, spending as much time as I could with my family, exercising when I could, and getting as much sleep as I could (in those days, my most frequent dreams were of sleeping). Now that I'm older, family and work are still very important to me and are at the top of my priorities, but I now have time for other things. The other day, I took time from writing this book to take a boat ride. There was time to do it. I also have more time to cultivate friendships and to renew ones that were forced by a busy schedule onto the back burner.

The point is that you need to define what balance means to you—and to focus on that balance.

Lee and King offer some good advice for achieving balance for the increasingly harried, whose daily lives depend on nothing going wrong in order to get everything done.

Integrating: Weaving into your life your various needs and activities. If you know what you want, then you can design time to accomplish your goals in an integrated way. This is in contrast to compartmentalizing your life, where you build in five minutes for healthy family table talk. Integration is going on a business trip and taking an extra two days at the end for vacation. Or an influential executive traveling with her small child and nanny allowing for evening quality time. This would have been unthinkable thirty years ago, but today's reality allows that integration of our work and life activities can help us get more from life.

Narrowing: Choosing what's most important and eliminating the non-essential. It's never easy, but it's absolutely essential. A middle-level executive in a consulting firm put it this way: "When I started out, if a colleague came to me needing advice for a problem he was working on at six o'clock, I would stay to help him, even if we worked past midnight. Obviously, I gained some motivational chits that way, but in the process my evening with my family was ruined. I soon learned that I could offer advice to a colleague working on a project but didn't need to get too involved. I've narrowed my activities, keeping my top priorities in mind."

Moderating: Setting limits on the time and energy you give to various tasks and roles. Setting limits acknowledges that everything doesn't have to be perfect. (We'll discuss later that you don't have to be great at everything.) Knowing that you don't have to be perfect can be very empowering. The house doesn't have to be perfectly clean; the child's sixth birthday party doesn't need to be an extravaganza. You don't always have to win at tennis.

Sequencing: Not trying to do all of the priorities at once. For example, Lee and King say, if work and family are very high priorities, and if early fall is an extremely busy time for work but November and December are less so, then plan accordingly. You'll be happy going full-tilt with your work, and you and your family will be happy spending more time together during the holidays.

Adding resources: Taking the pressure off by putting people, systems, and money to work for you. Susan, a highly skilled lawyer with two young children, had been working part-time so that she could meet her parenting responsibilities in her way while staying active in her profession. Recently offered a full-time position doing something that greatly interested her, she talked it over with the family. The children, now in elementary school, were less needy. But accommodations would have to be made. She would be earning a better income and, hence, able to pay others to take over jobs she now was doing herself. For example, instead of an outside housecleaner twice a month, she changed it to once a week. Instead of homemade meals each night, every other night was to be take-out, her husband would cook, or the family would go out to dinner. Shopping, household, and childcare duties were shared with her spouse. Too often, we have this need to take on new challenges, while making no other adjustments in our life.

We can add resources, we can sequence our activities, we can moderate them, we can narrow down our priorities, and we can find ways to integrate them. This is good advice from Lee and King.

Here is some of my own, hoping that it'll be as helpful. Reading books, including this one, and talking to mentors and friends are good. But in the end you need to decide how best to balance your life. These are my suggestions:

Know yourself. Gee, that's a surprise, isn't it? You've worked hard to read and internalize this book, and now, with a better sense of what's important to you, as well as your strengths and weaknesses, you're better able to set your priorities objectively. Knowing yourself makes that easier. It also allows you to test those priorities frequently. Often people's goals are too narrow. Instead of feeling happy when they achieve a goal such as becoming a top executive, they feel a sense of loss. They realize they had given up a lot of what they didn't know was important. So, keep working to know yourself better.

Set priorities. In addition to Lee and King's advice on setting priorities, let's also try it another way. Jot down what you believe is most important in your life. When your list is completed, prioritize it. That's step one.

Then, assume that you've been told that you have only one month to live. Now jot down the five things you would want to do before the month is up.

Next, assume that your life has been extended to one year. Now go through the same exercise, listing what is most important for you to attend to during that year. Finally, go through the same exercise as if you have ten years to live.

Now take a good look at what you've written, starting with your original set of priorities and then moving from one month to one year and finally to ten years.

If they're 100 percent the same—you'd do the same thing whether you had a month or ten years to live—then you have a good handle on what's most important to you. Most of us aren't that fortunate. If you're like 99 percent of us, you'll see differences: People facing death in a month will plan to spend more time with those most important to them and strengthening those relationships, than those who have a decade or more to live. Now try to reconcile these various differences and to rewrite your first priority statement. Maybe it's still the same as your original statement. But if you're truthful, you can modify it based on this exercise. This rewritten priority statement is something you should keep close to you, just like your code of ethics.

Setting priorities is the best way to deal with the balance question.

Acknowledge that you can't control everything. I often tell student-athletes how fortunate they are to participate in sports. They learn about the payoff that comes from hard work, the importance of teamwork, and—the most valuable lesson of all—that sometimes life isn't fair. The ball bounces the wrong way, the referee misses a call, you are sick for the big game and perform poorly. Accept that you can't control everything and deal with the disappointments that come your way. Some disappointments may be the result of things you do, or don't do. Learn from it. But some may be caused by events that you absolutely cannot control. Accept that and move on.

Conversely, take responsibility for the things you can control. Psychologists talk about locus of control—where you fit on a continuum running from believing that you have complete control to no control. As I said, none of us can keep everything, from acts of war to just plain bad luck, from entering our lives. On the other extreme are those who believe everything is outside their control. This is a nice, convenient way to avoid any responsibility. "The devil made me do it," is how comic Flip Wilson often explained some bizarre behavior. "I would have gotten an A but the teacher didn't like me" may be true or it may be a complete rationalization. Playing the lottery is a way to cede control to externalities. I'm not talking about someone who buys an occasional ticket, but someone who spends half of his paycheck hoping to win—even though the odds of a piano falling on his head are better. You need to accept responsibility for what, in fact, you can do. The Alcoholics Anonymous prayer is instructive: "God grant me the serenity to accept the things I cannot change; courage to change the things I can; and wisdom to know the difference."

Try to avoid unhappy or manipulative people. Sometimes you just can't; often you can. Being overly nice to them isn't worth your time because they will not reciprocate. Here are a few to avoid:

• Someone who credits his success solely to his brains and hard work, making no acknowledgment that being the boss's son might have helped a little. He often believes that anyone who isn't successful or who has suffered mishaps, even tragedies, deserves his lot in life. Something that the unfortunate person did or didn't do caused his pancreatic cancer or got him struck by lightning. Don't waste your time with such people.

• Someone who believes that everything in his life is a result of external factors. He'll bore you with each tale of woe, conspiracy, and bad luck. It's a real downer and you don't need it.

• Then take the difficult person, please. He's the guy who doesn't care about your opinion and doesn't want a relationship. He simply wants you to adopt his point of view or get you to do something he wants. He will suck up your time and emotional energy, and give you nothing in return.

You can add to this list yourself. The point is you don't have to be friends with everyone. It's important to treat people with respect, not rudeness. You don't have to be their friend. Stay away from people who make your life more difficult.

Find intimacy in your life. Perhaps it's a spouse, significant other, or a close friend. You'll be a happier person if you have someone you can confide in and who can confide in you—someone you can really trust. Occasionally you will dump your problems on that person, and just by listening, he or she will make you feel better. More often, the relationship itself is what will keep you going in stressful times. I've been fortunate to have as my wife and partner for more than forty years someone who shared my dreams for work, family, and community service. More important, she is someone I can call a close friend—someone I know will always be there for me. If you have no such relationship, try to find one, as there must be a big void in your life.

Find ways to serve others. This is one way you'll find a like-minded candidate for an intimate relationship. Public service, volunteer work, church activities, involvement in local and state government, or whatever—even an hour a week will make you a happier and better person. A colleague and friend, William Coplin, has written a guide to doing good deeds in your everyday life.[9] He makes clear that doing good things is nice and makes for a better world, but also makes you a better and happier person. The abundance of research convinces me that this is so. In return for your gift of time and friendship, you will receive the great gift of knowing that you've made a difference. Each of us has to decide how much energy to expend on serving others. But you'll be happier if it's incorporated into your balanced life.

Know that "good enough" sometimes really is "good enough." You don't have to be the best at everything you do. Your child won't be scarred for life if you don't have the world's greatest birthday party. If you are self-aware and prioritize, you'll decide not to do some things. My colleague Susan, who went from part-time to full-time lawyer, gave up a couple of community activities to ensure that her life remained balanced.

When our three children were growing up, my wife and I were both active at work and in community pursuits. We would have liked to have our children go to school in laundered and pressed clothing. Their clothing was always clean but not pressed. We joked that we would need to set aside time to teach them what an iron was, in case it was ever on an IQ test. We also insisted

9. William Coplin, *How You Can Help: An Easy Guide to Doing Good Deeds in Your Everyday Life* (New York: Routledge Press, 2000).

early on that they make their own lunch for school ("early on" means first grade). They were supervised, of course, at first. But soon no supervision was necessary. These weren't gourmet lunches, but we all survived.

In my life I learned early on that I had very little mechanical aptitude. In fourth grade a skills test showed that I was below average. It's sometimes frustrating to be unable to do mechanical things, but I have accepted it and either do them poorly or, usually, find someone else to do them. The latter approach makes my wife happy. Me too. Be happy doing some things just good enough so that you can do the important things very well.

Remind yourself that the fun of life is the chase, not the result. Few of us always achieve our goals. Sometimes they are unrealistic, sometimes we don't work hard enough, sometimes it just isn't in the cards. The chase is important. I've always felt that working to win and playing to win was most important in a competitive contest. I've never liked losing, but I can accept it if I'm working and playing to win. If I didn't like the work and the play, I would often be very unhappy, as I don't always get to win my tennis matches. It's the chase that must be fun for you. Remember my story about Warren Bennis, who loved being president but didn't love doing it? It's the doing that's most important. Former president Bill Clinton's image is that he greatly loved the chase—the campaigning, the long hours, the focus on policy positions, and dealing with emergencies. Had he lost his second election, he would of course have been greatly saddened. I have no doubt, however, that he would have felt the chase was worth it. He enjoyed it.

Contrast that with Al Gore. In his presidential campaign, did it ever appear that he loved the chase? From his public behavior, it would appear that the loss affected him very greatly. He sacrificed a great deal (perhaps because he didn't seem to love the chase) for something he didn't attain.

Remember, the fun of life is the chase.

Believe in something. I view myself as spiritual but not necessarily as a religious person. It helps that I believe in a god even though I'm not sure about any of the details. Some of you reading this are devout in your religion, some have weakly defined beliefs such as mine, some are agnostics, and some are atheists. I'm not telling you what to believe in. Rather, believing in something will help provide balance in your life. It may be a religious belief, it may be a belief in the way you want to conduct your life, or it may be belief in a cause or an individual. But believe in something. Ask yourself what you believe.

"Notice the difference when a man says to himself, 'I have failed three times' versus saying 'I am a failure.' It is the difference between sanity and self-destruction."

—S. I. Hayakawa

Try to find some humor in your life. Mundane activities can be very funny, if you open yourself up to the humor of them. I religiously read the comics, particularly *Dilbert* and *Doonesbury*. If I can start out the day with even a slight laugh, I'm happier. When I was in high school, I was on a basketball team that played in the finals of the state tournament. It was a stressful time for a seventeen-year-old. I remember picking up James Thurber's book *Thurber's Carnival*, leafing through it and getting engrossed in a story about Ohio State football in the 1940s. It had to do with a star lineman and his economics professor's efforts to keep him eligible. I started laughing and laughed to the point where I lost total control. This kept on for about ten minutes. I slept well that night. We still lost, but remember, it's the chase that matters. Laughter is very good medicine as long as it isn't a cruel attempt to demean others.

Forgive yourself for your mistakes. You already have learned that you can't take responsibility for things beyond your control. Understand that you will make mistakes. Analyze them, learn from them, and strive to do better. But forgive yourself. We all need to move on. Making mistakes is a part of being human. In fact, if we go through life afraid of making mistakes, we cannot achieve our potential.

Try to find a way to learn from setbacks. The fact is you will have them. The important thing is that you learn from them. Pulley and Wakefield[10] explain that hardships such as job losses, career setbacks, and other mistakes and failures are regarded as the key learning experiences by many failed executives. The key word here is resilience—having a sense of hope about the future regardless of the setback. Hardships are learned from "traveling through a valley of chaos" before resuming the climb. This is very painful but if we don't work through the pain, we remain stuck, generally feeling sorry for

10. Mary Lynn Pulley and Michael Wakefield, *Building Resiliency: How to Thrive in Times of Change*, (Greensboro, N.C.: Center for Creative Leadership, 2001).

ourselves. Not easy, but since we all have setbacks we need to learn from them and move on.

In this section, I've tried to show how I and others feel about securing balance. I've also offered you a way to set priorities about how you spend your time. It's now time for you to thoughtfully give yourself direction.

Self-Awareness Exercise. So, here is your assignment. Keep your completed priorities assignment close to you so that you can frequently refer to it as you make decisions about your time and what is most important to you.

Your Responsibility for Leadership Development in Others

> *Leaders who are adept at cultivating people's abilities*
> *show a genuine interest in those they are helping along,*
> *understanding their goals, strengths, and weaknesses.*
> *Such leaders can give timely and constructive feedback*
> *and are natural mentors or coaches.*
> —James M. Kouzes and Barry Z. Posner,
> *The Leadership Challenge*

> *Good leaders accept and act on the paradox of power:*
> *we become most powerful when we give our power*
> *away.*
> —James M. Kouzes and Barry Z. Posner,
> *The Leadership Challenge*

By now, you know that self-awareness is an important word to remember. Here's another that can't be said too often: *responsibility*. You took responsibility for learning and applying the material in this book. Each day you step into a leadership position, you accept the obligations of responsibility. Among them is helping others to become better leaders. The others are everywhere — your coworkers, subordinates, even family members. Whatever you do, you have a responsibility to help them learn and grow.

This brief section will focus on how to do just that. But, just like most of

what you learned, you'll have to adapt it to your own specific situation and make a commitment to apply it.

Writers in this area, such as DuBrin,[11] Lussier and Achua,[12] Kouzes and Posner,[13] and Goleman[14] offer some suggestions for promoting leadership. I'll summarize their views, and then I'll give you some specific take-home points. They recommend some or all of the following.

Create Rich Developmental Experiences for Coworkers

This would include such activities as 360-degree feedback, coaching, and mentoring.

11. Andrew J. DuBrin, *Leadership: Research Findings, Practice, and Skills*, 4th ed. (New York: Houghton Mifflin, 2004).

12. Lussier and Achua, *Leadership*.

13. Kouzes and Posner, *Leadership Challenge*.

14. Goleman, Boyatzis, and McKee, *Primal Leadership*.

360-degree feedback. Give your colleague feedback from a large number of people. It's called 360-degree feedback because it is expected that it will come from all corners, such as peers superiors, subordinates, and customers. This can be an excellent tool for personal and professional growth. However, it can be abused and turn counterproductive if the information received is not confidential to the person being evaluated or if it is used too frequently. But as a development tool, it can be very helpful, particularly if interpreting the results for your colleague is done sensitively and with true concern for his growth.

Coaching. Many of us have participated on athletic or other teams, or were at least required to take physical education in school. The athlete-coaching skills you saw then are now being used successfully in the business world; the focus is on maintaining and continually improving performance. This is done by providing motivational feedback aimed at improvement, not debasement. Lussier and Achua [15] offer ten coaching guidelines:

- Develop a supportive working relationship
- Give praise and recognition
- Avoid blame and embarrassment
- Focus on behavior, not the person
- Have employees assess their own performances
- Give specific and descriptive feedback
- Give coaching feedback
- Provide modeling and training
- Make feedback timely but flexible
- Don't criticize

Lussier and Achua remind us that harsh criticism just doesn't work. "If you must correct someone, never do it after the fact. Bite your tongue and hold off until the person is about to do the same thing again and challenge the person to make a more positive contribution." There's a fine line between offering helpful suggestions and being critical. I'm not sure I always know where that line is, nor should you feel you'll always be right when you coach. To hold back information denies people a chance to learn from their mistakes. To pound them in the ground with it makes them defensive.

Best to think about the least critical way of framing your coaching advice

15. Lussier and Achua, *Leadership*, 173.

before you dispense it. Then accept the fact that sometimes you may have been too subtle to be heard. Or that others took it so personally that it was never received.

Mentoring. This is coaching in which a more experienced person helps a less experienced protégé. In most cases, a mentor is not working with a direct report. Mentoring often involves giving good career advice and helping to improve leadership techniques and other skills. Since the protégé is not a direct report, he doesn't feel pressure to please the mentor, knowing that it doesn't lead to promotion or serious problems.

My guess is that different people have mentored you. Think about how the most effective people handled it; also think about those mentoring events that just weren't that helpful.

In sum, such developmental experiences as 360-degree feedback, coaching, and mentoring offer ways that you can assist in the development of people.

Give People Increasing Responsibilities

Provide a pathway to confidence and further development. Kouzes and Posner describe several studies dealing with competence and confidence. A study of the U.S. Navy's best ships revealed that their commanding officers gave priority to the development and growth of their crews. And studies of salespeople show persistence, likeability, and focus are key ingredients of success. Leaders spend a lot of time developing these qualities.

People who are given additional responsibility will, of course, make mistakes. But the good ones will learn from their mistakes, particularly with your guidance, and develop the competence and confidence needed to become better leaders. You, of course, will flourish each time another person has grown under your tutelage.

People have a better chance of being successful if you share information with them, explaining the context of the challenge you are giving them. Jack Stack, CEO of SRC Holdings, spends 86 percent of his company's training budget on educating everyone to be a businessperson. "If everyone has good information about what is happening in the business, then everyone, regardless of position, begins thinking like a CEO. My job gets easier."

Establish a Learning Climate

This is important, if you are a school, business, not-for-profit, or governmental entity. Syracuse University prides itself on being a learning community. This is more than teaching students. It involves a faculty growing in scholarship, and a staff improving each year and accepting responsibility for self-improvement. No one is excluded. Employees are allowed to attend classes, on their own time, at no expense to them. Many have received advanced degrees; they and we are the better for it. Our human resources department offers a plethora of programs each semester ranging from developing technology and leadership skills to learning day-to-day information parents need to do better. (Our employees' children also are allowed to attend classes free.)

Being a learning community, of course, is a morale booster, but this is not why we do it. We know that private universities are in a highly competitive environment. Each and every one of us must continue to grow, from the parking attendant to the chancellor. It works for Syracuse and for many other universities. It clearly works and is regularly employed in high tech and other knowledge-intensive firms. It can work in your environment.

And now, by way of summary, some specific suggestions for ensuring that your role in leadership development is effective.

- Give people increasingly challenging assignments.
- Dispense recognition when people do well. Offer them more than praise. Give them opportunities to display their effectiveness by, for example, having them make presentations when they have been heavily involved in their preparation. This builds the competence and confidence needed to grow.
- Deliver honest feedback. People don't grow if we ignore their weaknesses and mistakes. We try to do this, of course, in the least critical way.
- Share information. At Syracuse, we've tried to make our budget operation as transparent as possible, so everyone can understand the reasons for the decisions. The more information we provide, the more we set a context for events, the better everyone can join and grow with the team.
- Provide the formal and informal learning opportunities we've previously described.
- Really care about the growth and development of your colleagues. If

you do care, you'll show it by listening to them, learning about their goals, their reservations, and the like. And if you do care, you will ask them how you can contribute to their growth.

The bottom line is that leadership is self-awareness, taking responsibility, and, mostly, caring.

Reality Exercise. Think of a coworker that you could assist by coaching or mentoring. Describe how you could make it happen.

In one of your groups or organizations, devise a program that helps to make it a better learning community.

Close to the End

Make what you have learned a part of your everyday thinking. To help internalize what you've read, list your twenty most important lessons. I will model this for you by unveiling Buzz's Top Twenty. Afterwards, keep your Top Twenty in a handy folder for occasional reference.

Buzz's Top Twenty

1. I can be one of those people who make things happen. I can *do* leadership.

2. My chances of being a strong, intentional leader are enhanced by practicing the leadership skills in this book.

3. I can be a leader whether it is as a positional or an informal leader. It is up to me. I also can be a willing and effective follower.

4. I want to be a moral leader—one who not only motivates others to take action, but also insures that the difficult issues are tackled. This is the adaptive role of leaders.

5. I will work to become more self-aware. I can start by looking at myself—my strengths and weakness as they relate to performing the four functions of leaders.

6. I will use my understanding of the leadership frames (structural, human resources, political, and symbolic) to determine how I should lead and whether it is within my skill set and interests to do so.

7. Emotional intelligence separates the outstanding from the poor leaders; self-awareness is the key.

8. In just about every culture, trustworthiness, integrity, and justice are major expectations of leaders. Being an ethical leader is the right thing to do: it is also necessary if I want to stay a leader.

9. Knowing and applying the basic conflict-resolution skills of listening, repeating, indicating areas of agreement, and then of disagreement, are important and will take me a long way. But I must avoid seeing the zero-sum solution as the one that works best for me.

10. The best way to motivate others is to find out which motivational currencies people value, and then build up chits so that they will want to contribute.

11. Leadership is also about power. The sources of power—coercive, reward, legitimate, expert, and charismatic—all have a place, with coercion being the least effective. Both positional and informal leaders are able to influence when they effectively use the power sources available to them.

12. Decision making is both an art and a science. The key is to relate decisions to vision, mission, and values. Good decisions are usually legitimate when others are involved beforehand. Other keys to remember are using the discipline of tradeoffs and being transparent with information. Also, my intuition is important, but I need to keep in touch with opposing views because in some areas my intuition is way off base.

13. In times of crisis, I need to be highly visible and in control. People need to be praised, encouraged, and kept motivated in spite of their sleep deprivation. At the end of the crisis, I should distribute much praise but also push to ensure that every phase of the crisis intervention activity is evaluated so we will be more ready the next time.

14. As a leader, I must be a strong communicator. This involves much more than talking and writing well. I must be a good listener, establish trust and credibility, and repeat the "story" in as many different ways as possible.

15. Having group skills separates me from others who are trying to lead. By knowing the importance of group purpose and group size, strengthening my positive group roles, and remembering to use my meeting and creativity enhancing skills, I can make a real difference.

16. I can become an effective change agent if I focus on what is most im-

portant, use the skills I have already been taught, give people reasons to want to buy in, and give them the skills they will need.

17. I can be more successful as a leader if I acknowledge the importance of understanding cultural differences and if I make an honest effort to understand and appreciate the important contributions that others can make.

18. I will behave ethically, otherwise people won't trust me. I will use my own code of behavior to guide my actions. I know I won't always make the right choices, but I will try.

19. Leaders maintain some balance in their lives. I must set priorities and spend my time, as best I can, consistent with those priorities. In some cases, I will have to settle for "good enough." I will also accept the things outside my control and move on.

20. Finally, I will work to help others develop their leadership potential.

The End: Self-Assessment

The Top Twenty exercise reminds you of what you've learned. But as I have said before, I also want you to have a better understanding of yourself and to have a greater ability to use your new skills. You can assess your self-understanding and the application of your new skills with the next two exercises.

> **Skills Self-Examination.** Have you strengthened any of the skills you have been learning? I have provided a before-and-after exam for you to decide just how much progress you have made since starting this book.

I provide these last minute annoyances to help you determine just how much progress you have made, and to remind you of a very important point: You are never finished learning and improving. While our journey together is over, your journey continues. How far you want to go as an intentional leader will be entirely up to you. Remember, it's the chase that's important. Good luck to you in your life's work.

Skills Self-Examination

Please rank your skill level as:
    1 (low)
    2 (moderate)
    3 (medium)
    4 (high)
    5 (superior)

Skill	*Before*	*After*
My ability to develop a plan to improve my skills in an area I want to strengthen	_____	_____
My tenacity in carrying out a skills development plan	_____	_____
My willingness to evaluate the results of my skills development efforts	_____	_____
My ability to use the motivational currencies effectively to achieve a "buy in"	_____	_____
My ability to use conflict-resolution techniques effectively	_____	_____
My ability to use group size and purpose effectively	_____	_____
My ability to use positive group roles	_____	_____
My ability to bring out creativity in groups	_____	_____
My ability to learn about other cultures and to "do business" with my new colleagues	_____	_____
My ability to recognize the stages of organizational grief and to move the stages along to successful completion	_____	_____
My ability to have a personal ethical code to guide me in my dealings with others	_____	_____
My ability to develop a statement of life's priorities	_____	_____
My ability to plan and execute a program to develop leadership in others	_____	_____

Appendixes

Index

Appendix A

Challenging Questions/ Short Answers

I asked students and other colleagues to read an early manuscript and to ask practical questions inspired by their reading. The answers to these questions are brief to keep them interesting. Consider them a start in dealing with issues that are far more complex than I am making them. Good leaders learn how to fill in the blanks.

Leadership Defined and Explained

QUESTION: I am confused. What is the difference between task 3, "implementing mission, goals, and values," and task 4, "serving as the keeper of the mission, goals, and values"?

ANSWER: Warren Bennis best describes the difference. Task 3 is doing things right—the all-important management function. It is getting the job done, with the help of others, of course. Task 4 is doing the right things. Good leaders have to do both. Some outstanding managers can never get to this point. The ones that do become the "conscience" of their organization and are true leaders

Self-Awareness and Emotional Competence

QUESTION: Should a leader take credit for accomplishments on his watch or defer praise to others?

ANSWER: Both. It is always best to offer generous praise to the entire team when there is a team effort and to other individuals when you and a colleague have successfully completed a task. Because you are part of the team, you will get your share of the credit, particularly if you are generous with your praise. But, you might ask, "what if my boss doesn't understand my role in making our project a success?" It is appropriate for you along the way to keep your boss apprised of what is going on and to seek her counsel on strategy, making clear the important role that you played.

QUESTION: When I read this chapter and do the self-awareness exercises, I am humbled by my several weaknesses. If I am not really good at all these things, can I really lead?

ANSWER: Congratulations. You have passed the first test of leadership. You are beginning to know and understand yourself. You can improve on your weaknesses if you dedicate yourself to doing so. You can also surround yourself with people who compensate for them. A self-aware, emotionally intelligent person isn't threatened by having people on the team better than he is at some things. But remember and use your strengths. Your strong points are what will make you successful. In other words, acknowledge and build on your weaknesses, but play to your strengths.

QUESTION: Whenever I get involved in a new activity, I begin to wonder if the uncertain payoff will merit my efforts. This often leads me to procrastinate and eventually give up without ever really getting engaged. How can I motivate myself?

ANSWER: Maybe you are too quick to say you will get involved. Some of your procrastination may be because you really aren't that interested. If you start out really interested, try setting short- and medium-term goals to achieve. This will give you more immediate results and keep you on target. If you always procrastinate, then pick something and push yourself to finish before you even consider another project.

QUESTION: How do you know the right balance for being a structural, human resource, political, and symbolic leader?

ANSWER: The proper balance depends on two things: your strengths and interests, and the situation. You learn about the former by becoming more self-aware and the latter by observing the situation before you act. If you are an aspiring politician, you know that the political and symbolic frames are required. If you are leading a group of computer experts, the human resources and structural frames might work best. The other part, your interests and strengths, require that you surround yourself with people who are better at the frames that aren't your strong points. How do you know the proper balance? Observation, trial and error, and constant evaluation of yourself and how you are doing.

Conflict Resolution

QUESTION: What do you do as a boss when people are forever arguing over small points, coming to you with their views, and denouncing the other person's ideas and overall ability?

ANSWER: Here's a story. In one situation, I had two people who really didn't like each other. More important, they had a legitimate disagreement over what should be included in a new human resources policy. Being eager to please, I listened patiently to each person far longer than I should have. I then invited them in together and asked each to give his/her viewpoints. I noticed absolutely no eye contact between them during their presentations. It was also clear that they hadn't talked much to each other. When the two had finished, I pounded on the table and said, "I've never seen such irresponsible and unprofessional behavior. The two of you can't even look at each other. I expect you to be able to work together, whether you like each other or not. Now, I've spent far too much time with each side of the issue. I want the two of you to leave now, get together to discuss your various views, identify what you agree to, and the areas that remain unresolved. You can write it up, and I will resolve the unresolved areas in fifteen minutes."

Now, no one wants his superior to resolve such a complex issue in fifteen minutes! In any event, they left, and a week later they sent me a joint letter that indicated total agreement. They had done a good job. They also didn't want me to resolve something in fifteen minutes because "I didn't know nearly as much as they did about the issue." They were right.

In short, the take-home lesson here is: (1) Don't let each side dump on the other privately to you; (2) tell them you want to know what they agree with and what they disagree with; and (3) warn them that you'll resolve any disagreement in fifteen minutes. The rest takes care of itself. I have used this technique for over thirty years; I occasionally have had to resolve differences, but not often.

QUESTION: What if the person uses dirty tricks such as personal attacks?

ANSWER: Don't fall for it. Remember, it's the issue not the person. Simply letting the person know that you're not taking the bait will help move things along.

QUESTION: What if a person simply will not budge?

ANSWER: Here's where you can indicate that the two of you can push the problem upstairs—using the approach that Terry mentioned—But don't do this until you've honestly worked through the issues. Both of you know the downside to pushing it up if you haven't worked hard to resolve it. However, knowing it can be pushed up often moves you and your colleague to resolution.

QUESTION: This four-step approach to conflict resolution seems so stilted. Why do I feel so uncomfortable when I follow the steps?

ANSWER: Once you get good at it, you don't have to follow each step. Also, the more you work with an individual, the less you need to repeat what is said. Seldom, however, will you acquire the kind of relationship where you can eliminate the third step, indicating areas of agreement. It doesn't take that long to do it, and it sets the stage for getting to a positive decision.

QUESTION: Whenever I am in a conflict situation, I just back off. It makes me nervous to push back. What should I do?

ANSWER: You don't have to push back. Remember, if you use the four steps, you will be working toward a mutually acceptable solution. Most often, you will find that the other person also wants to find something about which you can both agree. If you don't engage, you will be ignored. Over time, that will be even more stressful for you. Practice the four steps, and you will begin to feel more comfortable finding common ground.

QUESTION: When I try to use the conflict resolution technique of repeating back what the person has said, I sometimes feel that I am being patronizing and making them even more hostile. What should I do?

ANSWER: Because it is a new skill, you may be too literal in your repeating. Try to say what the person means rather than his exact words. This takes time and practice, but don't give up. However, if you are really making them more hostile, cut back on the times you paraphrase, and show you understand through nodding and other body language. If that doesn't work, ask for a cooling-off period. The hostility may need to simmer before anything constructive can be accomplished. If the hostility is meant to manipulate you into agreement, you need to confront the person, letting him know you want to work things out but that certain ground rules of behavior will need to be established.

QUESTION: In conflict situations, how do you deal with someone who is completely closed to any opinion other that her own?

ANSWER: If the issue is unimportant, drop it. It isn't worth your time. If it is important, discuss the person's inflexibility with her and suggest as a ground rule that all views should receive a respectful hearing. Avoid making it personal. If this doesn't work, bump the decision to a higher level, if there is one. If not, agree to disagree, and try to avoid having to deal with the person. Try to stay on good terms because perhaps the person will read this book. (Probably not.) They only know the zero-sum game, and you don't need to be their patsy.

Motivating Others

QUESTION: The idea of currencies is interesting, but how do you know which ones to use on a specific person?

ANSWER: First, get to know the person—the real person. Listen and observe to form an opinion as to what might be the best motivator. Second, understand enough about the culture of the group to know what motivates most of the people in that group. What do they talk about? What gives them pride? Third, try one or more of the currencies based on what you have learned. If it works, you are home free. If it doesn't, try something else until you hit the jackpot.

QUESTION: I am a supervisor of a small work group. One of the workers does just enough to get by and sometimes less than that. I have tried all of the currencies and certain ones work for a short time, then it is back to subpar performance. What should I do?

ANSWER: Maybe the person has personal problems. Maybe he doesn't like his work. Maybe he doesn't like you. Nice to know, but you still need to expect better performance. Tell him your expectations; find out if there are ways you can help him be more productive. Use the currencies that work best for him, and if all of this fails—don't make it your problem. You have someone who is holding everyone else back. Leaders sometimes have to let people go. Perhaps you could have done a better job of motivating him, but it doesn't matter. He has to go.

QUESTION: Is it possible that I could focus so much on using the motivational currencies that the organization loses site of its goals? Could I be making things worse rather than better?

ANSWER: Not if you remember that the currencies are only tools—means to achieving the organization's goals. If you are using the currencies properly, you should see goal achievement. If there doesn't seem to be progress, perhaps you are using the wrong currencies. If nothing seems to work, get your group together and ask them what the problem is and what needs to be done to get back on track.

QUESTION: When motivating those who have relationship needs, what do you do if others feel that you are playing favorites?

ANSWER: It is likely that those motivated by other currencies, such as task or inspirational, won't be that concerned if you are giving them what they need. Be sure you are. It is possible that there are others in the group with less obvious relationship needs who are your problem. Try giving them a little relationship time. Also, ask yourself what your motivational needs are. If your relationship need is the strongest, you may have gone overboard in this area. It is important to be aware of how people are reacting, and you have made a good start by acknowledging that a proper balance is necessary.

The Power That Can Be Yours

QUESTION: Are charismatic leaders always persistent?

ANSWER: Some are, some aren't. Good leaders are very persistent regardless of how charismatic they are. Good charismatic leaders persist and surround themselves with people that see that things are carried out. They also have the good sense to know when to change direction. Poor charismatic leaders give little attention to the implementation part of leadership and are all too eager to let the momentum die so long as they can find a new platform to stand on.

QUESTION: What is most important for a leader to be: liked, feared, respected, or smart?

ANSWER: All are important although fear is the least important. As you have learned, coercive power has major limitations over time. Leaders are usually smart (especially emotionally competent), and tend to be liked—but not always. To me, the most important by far is respect. Leaders earn the respect of others; people we respect, we will follow.

QUESTION: My situation is very difficult. My boss gives me great performance reviews and tells me I am his most valuable person. Yet, when we are in group situations, he challenges my comments and often belittles me. What should I do?

ANSWER: He respects your work, or he wouldn't be giving you good performance reviews. Perhaps he likes to challenge his best person. Perhaps your group skills are lacking. Maybe you are too sensitive. Maybe he is threatened in some way when the two of you are in a group. The point is, you don't know. Approach your boss and bring up the subject of the disconnect between your positive reviews and his reactions to you in a group. Do so in a positive way; ask him if there is something you are doing wrong when you are in group situations. He will probably tell you. Then continue using your expert power, and you will continue to be valuable.

QUESTION: How do I know if I am using my power effectively?

ANSWER: Remember the definition—the ability to get others to take the action you want. Usually you will know whether this is happening; however, this is where your self-awareness skills can be very helpful.

QUESTION: Acquiring power can help you to lead. But it seems manipulative—wrong to me. What am I missing?

ANSWER: Remember, all of the skills you have learned can be used for good or for evil. Your power can be an ethical tool. If you have doubts in a given situation, question your motivation—your reasons for using power. If you are uncomfortable with your motivation, then move on. However, sometimes, excessive introspection is a way to avoid doing something.

QUESTION: If someone in a leadership position above you is abusing her power, what do you do?

ANSWER: If the person can do you harm, tread lightly. Perhaps you can make suggestions for improving the situation; never make it personal. Keep careful notes of conversations and actions by the person and, above all, maintain you integrity. Eventually she will fall, and you don't want to be taken down with her. If the person can't do you harm, confront the issue directly, again without making it personal. Focus on behavior, not the person. The four-step approach to conflict resolution might be helpful. If you feel that your efforts are in vain, you can decide whether to take the issue further, drop it, or drop out.

QUESTION: What if I'm on a project committee outside the chain of command? How can I obtain influence over others?

ANSWER: This situation is becoming frequent in today's corporate world and elsewhere. John Kotter believes that this is where most of the power gap is—where things get done outside the chain of command. To Kotter, the ability to use power depends on identifying where all the relevant lateral relationships exist—asking the question "whom do I need to influence?" It means developing good relationships with these people (human exchange) so that you're able to communicate and influence them, or to negotiate when necessary. Further, it means looking for the mutuality of interests—finding things in common to build on rather than assuming that disagreement makes us enemies. Of course, the use of expert power comes into play with the ability to use information channels, to control resources, and to establish a track record of demonstrated expertise.

Decision Making: An Art and a Science

QUESTION: Do leaders only deal with the tough decisions?

ANSWER: Leaders need to be involved in the big decisions and the small ones that could cause big problems if not handled well. Leaders must also insure that people understand how a given decision will be made—who is to be involved, what the time frame is, and ultimately who will make the decision. Finally, whether or not the leader makes the tough decision, she must stand ready to support it and the people who were involved in making it. Leaders take most of the blame when things go badly and generously share the credit when it turns out well.

QUESTION: You make it sound as though many people should have input before you make a decision. How do you determine who and how many need to be involved?

ANSWER: Ask your self two questions: (1) Who is needed because of their expertise? (2) Who is needed to make the decision legitimate? The groups aren't necessarily the same, but you need to attend to both. Sometimes a large number is needed; sometimes, by necessity, only a few. And sometimes there isn't time to consult. In such cases, you just need to make a decision and explain it afterwards. I said earlier that decision making is both an art and a science. This is the art part.

QUESTION: Doesn't asking large numbers of people for input before you make a decision just make them angry and cynical when you don't follow their suggestions?

ANSWER: Maybe. But look at it this way. People would rather be consulted than completely left out. As long as you explain your decision and the reasons for it, they will feel better than if you just spring it on them. Of course, each would prefer that you do exactly what he recommends. Ah, the burdens of leadership!

QUESTION: At work, whenever I make a bad decision, I get slammed by my boss. It makes me not want to stick out my neck again. What should I do?

ANSWER: I don't blame you. Maybe it is your boss's problem. Some bosses like to play the "gotcha" game. It masks their insecurities. First, know your boss. If she wants to be involved in every decision, know that. If she gives you flexibility but slams you when you are wrong, accept blame and move on. But have a conversation with your boss to get her views of how you might have handled things better. And then when you are boss, remember to empower your employees and help them to grow from their mistakes.

QUESTION: I want to follow the suggestion "Don't sweat the small stuff," but I worry that if I let little decisions go because they seem too small to make a difference, these small issues will build up and will eventually create a problem that could have been avoided. How should I deal with this worry?

ANSWER: Best bet is to stop worrying, and accept that you can't do everything. If you try to, you will end up worrying about not having enough time for the most important things. Know that sometimes you will wish that you had attended to a small matter, but that it's a calculated risk you take. Accept that you will sometimes make a mistake, and move on. If a small decision keeps bugging you, make it; but don't make a habit of doing it. When tempted, say to yourself, "I have more important things to work on now. Maybe I will or won't get back to it. This is the best way for me to spend my time at this moment."

The Leader as a Communicator

QUESTION: How do you communicate bad news—say a 20 percent reduction in staff?

ANSWER: First, think about the people you must tell. What will be their major concerns ("What does it mean to me?") and what do they need to hear to deal with the first step of the grieving process? Second, be honest and straightforward in explaining the situation. If you don't know, say you don't know. Third, explain the process—what will happen next, how decisions will be made, and the time frame for making them. Fourth, let them ask questions and vent, and show some empathy for their situation (and perhaps yours). They won't be happy, but they can respect the way you handled things.

QUESTION: I write well and am very articulate in one-on-one situations. But when I get up to speak, my hands sweat, and I know people can tell I am nervous. Should I forget about being a good speaker?

ANSWER: Remember the routine—practice, use visual imagery, and evaluate your practice sessions. If you are doing this twice now before speaking, do it four times. And when you get up to speak, visualize your audience in their winter pajamas. This will help you relax. It will also remind you that they aren't perfect, either.

QUESTION: As a leader, what do you do if you are in a situation where you are having real trouble communicating because of language and/or cultural barriers?

ANSWER: First, know your group going in (this should not be a surprise to you). You should learn what you can before going to the meeting. You could bring some one along to translate, but that isn't an optimal situation. In any event, you should apologize for your inadequacy and say that it is your problem—that you hope they will be patient with you. Better yet, don't put yourself in that position. It will be very difficult for you to lead.

Leading in Times of Crisis

QUESTION: My hero is Rudy Giuliani. The way he handled the September 11th aftermath was outstanding. Do you agree?

ANSWER: Yes, but he would be the first to admit that he had much help. He showed leadership by inspiring people under great stress and pulling people together. But there were thousands of leaders—police, firemen, emergency crews, logistics people, etc. As a leader, he should be proud. We should all be proud that so many people stepped forward.

QUESTION: What if a crisis situation arises and, as a leader, I do not possess the resources or funding to deal with it properly? What should I do?

ANSWER: Call your group together. Get an accurate definition of the problem. See if they have suggestions. Do the same with people you respect who may have contacts. See if they have suggestions about whom to contact. Do all of this quickly, and farm out the crisis to those you have identified as better able to deal with it. It is always a blow to the ego to confront the reality that you can't do everything, but it is true. You will have done the right thing.

Leading Groups

QUESTION: I chair a meeting where everyone wants to talk—usually not about what brought us together. It is fun for a while, but nothing gets done. Any advice to offer?

ANSWER: You need to confront this with the group. But first, be sure that you have planned the meeting well and that everyone knows the purpose. Second, before the next meeting, go over the positive group roles section and practice some of them so that you can use them. After the meeting, use the evaluation time to talk about the need to stay focused. Ask people what they think the problem is. If it is you, find out how you can be more effective. Or perhaps they just need some education about how to behave in a group. You could go over the positive group roles with them to help them see how they can make a better contribution. Also, talk with members individually to get their buy in to having more productive meetings. It's a lot of work, but if you do nothing, these meetings will drive you crazy.

QUESTION: When dealing with unfamiliar people or large groups, I often find my personality changing from assertive and confident to quiet and reserved. How can I prevent this from happening?

ANSWER: You've already taken the first step by identifying something you want to change. The next step is to observe others who you feel show great confidence in large groups, then visualize how you will act the next time you are in that situation. Practice the visualization a half-dozen times. Then go out and field test your new approach. Afterwards, think about what worked, what didn't, and how you felt. Learn from the experience; visualize what you will do the next time and do it. Try it ten times. You may not become a social butterfly, but I bet that you will have far greater confidence and will feel much better about yourself. And you don't have to be a social butterfly. Be your new self.

QUESTION: In my experience with small groups, when I follow the positive role of taking initiative and setting standards for the group, I become the one to whom everyone looks for guidance, and I end up shouldering much of the responsibility for the group's activities. What should I do?

ANSWER: Spend more of your time in the group asking the opinions of others. This leads to greater buy in and, it is hoped, involvement on their part. You can also use an appropriate time in the meeting, beginning or end, to suggest that when decisions are made by the group, the work be spread around — the obligation is both to attend and participate in the meetings and to do the work. Also, you can say no when asked to take something on. People will know that you are busy. Finally, if nothing works, decide if involvement in the group is worth your time.

QUESTION: If I choose to use the Delphi approach to deal with a medium-sized or large group, I run the risk that many people don't respond to a mailing or to their e-mail. With a limited number of responses, I can't be sure that the entire group is represented fairly. How should I deal with this?

ANSWER: It's a problem that plagues even the best researchers. Make sure your opening remarks are interesting, and appeal to their sense of obligation. Also, try to make it fun, and make your directions easy to follow. You could offer a reward as some pollsters do (I wouldn't). If there is a small response, you can conclude the following: (1) the response is so small that I can't conclude anything; (2) those that don't respond aren't very heavily invested in the issue, so I can either do what is suggested by the few or just forget about it.

Before giving up on the seemingly uninterested, you might try sending them the comments and priorities from those who participated, and ask them to state agreement or disagreement with each suggestion. This will only take five minutes of their time, so you might get better participation.

QUESTION: Is there a way to tell if your task/socioemotional ratio is not achieving the strongest output before it is too late? For example, are there signs before people start to get crabby because they are being worked to hard, or before they get impatient because the group is too socioemotional?

ANSWER: Yes, and you have mentioned two of them. Also, after each meeting, ask the group for suggestions for improvement to make the next meeting even more productive and satisfying. If you get no helpful responses, seek out some of the members individually and ask the same question. Stay alert and encourage feedback and you stand a good chance of being successful.

QUESTION: What would be a good way to bring the different backgrounds of people in a work place to everyone's attention? Is there a way to get everyone to be more accepting of one another to break down racial and sexual barriers?

ANSWER: The best way is to run good meetings, stay focused on the task at hand, and encourage all to participate. Tolerance and acceptance come when people work as colleagues toward a common purpose. In such an environment, team members are appreciated for the value they add to the group. If there are varying agendas, or if some people aren't adding value, or if people adding value aren't recognized for their efforts, then creating a more tolerant and accepting environment will be very difficult.

QUESTION: If a small group cannot generate ideas that are good enough to move a company or group forward, should the leader bring in more people so there is more creativity and possibly more "piggybacking" and "leapfrogging"?

ANSWER: First, critique the sessions to determine if better facilitation is needed. Did the facilitator insure that no evaluative comments were tolerated? Did she encourage all to participate? Was the problem clearly stated? Next, ask the group for suggestions to improve the creative process, and do the same with individuals in the group. If you still feel that the ideas aren't good enough, bring in outside help. But give your group another chance first.

Diversity

QUESTION: I run a medium-sized business. How do I help my predominately white employees learn to be more tolerant and to work with all kinds of people?

ANSWER: First, be a good example. Your tolerance and appreciation of diverse groups shows more than you think, as does your ability to do business with people different from you. Second, in your hiring practices, try to obtain a more diversified workforce, and encourage your direct reports to do the same. Evaluating them on their effectiveness in recruitment and retention is a good motivator. Third, make it clear that your high performance standards apply to all. Your old employees need to hear that no favoritism will occur; your new employees will be grateful, as they won't want to be treated as special. Finally, in some cases, racial and cultural sensitivity training can help; it has to be good, however, and many aren't that helpful. Even if you have picked a good program, it won't help if the first three suggestions aren't followed. In other words, walk the talk.

QUESTION: I want to be more inclusive and work productively with all kinds of people. However, I keep putting my foot in my mouth. Am I hopeless?

ANSWER: Not hopeless, but maybe clueless. First, start reading about the cultures of people to which you are making the biggest gaffs. Second, when you do say something insensitive, apologize. Third, try to learn from your work colleagues. Admit your lack of knowledge and willingness to learn. People will respect you if you are trying and seen as fair and willing to learn.

QUESTION: I am a person of color. My white colleagues expect me to be up on the latest rap music and to provide the "black perspective" about various social issues. I went to a suburban high school and, rightly or wrongly, I don't have opinions on many of the things they ask me. Should I let it bug me?

ANSWER: No. They are probably well meaning, but even if they aren't, engage in those conversations that interest you. Bring up topics that deviate from what appears to be their stereotype of you. Also, when you can educate them, do so. Who knows, they may work for you some day.

QUESTION: At my university, I notice that the international students tend to congregate. Why are they so cliquish?

ANSWER: We all like to be with people that make us feel comfortable. International students are no different. You will find that as they become more comfortable with their new surroundings, they will socialize with others more. Also, because they look different, they are more noticed. Help the situation along by befriending a foreign classmate. You will grow from the experience.

Organizational Change

QUESTION: Is it okay to have fun?

ANSWER: Yes, in fact it is better than okay. One thing I often hear about good leaders is that it is fun to work with them. As people go through the stress and long hours that accompany change, having fun will make everything easier. You can make it fun by helping people understand that enjoying the change process is a good thing, and by not getting testy when you believe that fun has gotten in the way of progress. Just relax and have fun, but keep people focused.

QUESTION: I run a fairly large organization in great need of change. There is a group of employees who are vocalizing their opposition and doing worse behind the scenes. What should I do?

ANSWER: Let's go back to what you have learned. First, be sure you are giving enough support to those that have already bought into the need for change. Second, spend a great deal of time with the fence sitters—those who could support the program if it makes sense to them and if they think it will actually happen. Third, isolate the malcontents. If you are able, this is not a bad time to bring out what you have learned about coercive power. Firing one of the people will probably bring the others in line. Most important, stay the course. If you waffle or spend all of your time courting the malcontents, you are through.

QUESTION: Group creativity—I don't buy it. I find that one person, usually me, can come up with more and better ideas than any group. What am I missing?

ANSWER: Congrats, Einstein. Much of the problem is, as you have learned, that leaders don't know how to get groups to think creatively. Perhaps you could use your superior brainpower to learn how to conduct such meetings, and give it a try. Usually, but not always, effectively run groups can be more creative than individuals. It is possible that you are that exception. It is also possible that you need to reread the section on leading groups to greater creativity and do some practicing.

QUESTION: How does an organization know it needs to change?

ANSWER: Most organizations don't, and that is the problem, because most need to be positioned for change. Let's look at three ways to describe organizations in need of change.

1. Organizations that merely need to improve continually to stay at the top of their game. A for-profit example is a company that has good bottom line results and high investor confidence. If it doesn't allow for continuous improvement and a careful monitoring of the external environment, it can easily fall behind. The big danger here is complacency. "We are doing well, so why worry?" No doubt the Big Three U.S. automobile manufacturers said that fifty years ago.

2. Organizations that are losing ground or are barely keeping pace with the competition. Mere continuous improvement won't do it. Major change is needed. In the not-for-profit sector, the recent history of local United Ways provides an example. They got by for decades by incrementally giving out money to the agencies—the service providers. In the past decade or so, money has become tighter and social needs have greatly increased, which has meant that tinkering with the distribution of monies wasn't enough. Local United Ways had to start from scratch, analyzing community needs and distributing dollars to the highest-priority areas, often in spite of agency pressure to preserve the status quo. The successful ones continue to enjoy community support; those stuck on a status quo model have found that communities find new and different ways to support needs that the United Way distribution system ignores.

3. Organizations that require major transformational change to maintain viability. Certainly, the Bell telephone system saw this need, experiencing intense competition not only from other telephone providers but also from the internet and wireless alternatives. Anything less than transformational change means extinction.

Let me summarize my answer in this way. Don't make the mistake of low-balling your change needs. If you think continuous improvement will do it, think major change. If you think major change is needed, think transformation. If the need is for transformation, don't waste time, get moving! Thinking change beyond what most people believe is needed will put you ahead of the game—at least for today.

QUESTION: If doing the right thing is to my advantage, why do I see so many people who break the rules getting ahead?

ANSWER: Remember, keep your sights on the long haul. Our friend Mr. Kushe probably agreed with your position at one time. Unethical people can be successful, but can they provide sustained leadership? I don't think so. If your idea is to achieve short-run gains regardless of the cost to your integrity, follow Mr. Kushe's example. If you want to lead, follow your value system.

QUESTION: What about office romance?

ANSWER: If you don't remember anything else, remember—complexity. It is difficult to generalize about office romances, but I will try to break it down for you. There are three things to remember: (1) Office romance adds complexity to any workplace situation. It never makes things easier for the loving couple or for others affected by the situation. (2) It is quite rare to see an office romance actually enhance either party's career advancement (doesn't always hurt but rarely helps). (3) If you think that an office romance is for you, be sure you have your personal and professional priorities in order. The situation isn't to be taken lightly.

I am going to elaborate on one of these points—complexity. Note that there is a continuum of office relationships and the complexities they bring to the situation. The more complex, the more problematic for you and your partner.

1. Husband and wife—or other partners—working in the same unit or in close proximity. This is becoming increasingly common in business and has been so in government and education for some time. It can work if those involved behave professionally and have worked through the complex issues that could lead to problems. From personal experience, I know this can work. Still, it adds a level of complexity to the work environment.

2. Same-level colleagues where neither person has power over the other. Those involved may or may not be in the same unit, but frequent professional interaction occurs. This is a bit more complex but can be worked out. It is more risky than the first possibility, but intelligent people can find a way to work through potential conflicts of interest. Just don't be shocked when you find out that everyone knows about your not-so-well-kept secret.

3. A person in power who is attracted to an employee who shares the attraction. There are occasional happy endings, but the complexity level has increased greatly. What happens if the romance fizzles? Was this once-hot relationship really sexual coercion? Perceptions change over time, particularly if the breakup is one-sided. Or, consider the incident at Boeing, where the CEO was released because his relationship with an employee "caused embarrassment" to the organization. Be sure you know what you are doing.

4. A person in power wants a relationship with an employee who is not interested in him. This is far more complex, and the potential for problems is huge. First, after rejecting the boss's advances, perhaps the employee now feels that she is being treated worse than other employees, and the turndown of her much desired promotion was because she rejected him. Or, what if the employee agrees to the relationship out of fear of jeopardizing her job? Both bring the possibility of litigation and other deserved negative consequences. Not good.

5. The smitten boss makes a fool of herself in spite of the employee's attempts to keep the relationship professional. The boss, off the deep end, will probably not be around long. Expect a lawsuit. Definitely not good.

In short, know yourself and your work and professional priorities. Only you can decide matters of the heart. Just know you are adding complexity to your life and that of your partner. And be big enough to accept the fallout if things don't go well.

QUESTION: What about office romances where one or both of the parties are already married or otherwise committed?

ANSWER: This is even more complex and problematic. From a leadership perspective, assume that everyone knows that something is going on. Also, assume that people know that one or both of the parties are married. And assume that people are thinking and talking about whether the leader can be trusted if he so easily betrays the trust of someone who was or still is close to him. Finally, assume that they will be thinking, "Is this a person I can trust? Or will I also be betrayed?" A few leaders can overcome this; but don't plan on being the exception.

Living a Balanced Life

QUESTION: Setting priorities on my time and eliminating the nonessentials really works for me. But I have great difficulty in saying no when I am asked to help or be involved. How can I prioritize?

ANSWER: This is a problem that most of us have. If you have already set priorities, it becomes much easier. If you are like Terry, you might decide to give the person a few hours but draw the line at further involvement. Or, perhaps you can't or simply don't want to do even that. Then I suggest you say: "I am sorry, but I am already over-committed and have had to cut back on a number of things already. I just don't have the time." You will be nervous the first time, so visualize and practice as I have taught you. Most people will be understanding and respect your honest response. Those that don't aren't your problem unless it is your boss or someone else you need to rely on. Then you need to consider your priorities. For the rest, remember: not everyone needs to love you.

QUESTION: It is easy to talk about living a balanced life. Consider my world: I am taking night classes, I work a sixty-hour-a-week job, and I have three kids. I am just trying to make it through each day. Help.

ANSWER: If this is any consolation, you aren't alone. Please reread the section on balance. Go back over the priorities exercise. Are there things you are doing that, compared to your physical health and sanity, are less important? If so, rearrange your activities. Maybe you must work those long hours to buy more things, and you are confusing wants and needs. And maybe your situation will not change for a while. If so, reread what I have said about diet, sleep, and exercise. Yours is a common complaint. Only you can provide an answer that works for you. I admire your effort. Don't give up.

Your Responsibility for Leadership Development in Others

QUESTION: Does mentoring or coaching have to be a formal relationship?

ANSWER: No, it doesn't. When you work side by side with colleagues, there is ample opportunity to help them grow as employees and people. They will let you know if they are receptive to your guidance. They are the ones who have the most potential for growth. Formal arrangements are great because everyone knows the game plan, but most of us were informally coached and mentored before anyone knew what to call it. In other words, each situation is different.

QUESTION: I mentored a colleague for two years. He just got the promotion I was hoping for. Was I a fool?

ANSWER: No, you were a good teacher and mentor. These things happen, but not often.

Appendix B

To the Teacher

Here are a number of ways to use this book in the classroom, for independent study courses, and for in-service training programs.

1. A course that contains a number of topics with leadership as a part of the course content. You might use parts of the book that fit in best with what you want to accomplish. For example, you might want to include chapter 2, leadership defined and explained, along with certain skill development topics such as conflict resolution, motivating others, running a meeting, and communications. Or you might want to combine chapter 2 with a heavy dose of self-awareness and ethics. I designed the book in this way to allow you to pick and choose, although I believe chapter 2 is an essential part of any combination used.

2. A course in leadership for undergraduate students. You might use the entire book and require all or most of the exercises. Classroom activities might focus on the exercises and skill development. Outside requirements might include additional readings and/or activities. Community and public service requirements fit perfectly into this scheme.

3. A course in leadership taught for advanced undergraduate or graduate students in any number of disciplines. I suggest using the book as the basic text and supplementing it with other readings in the specific area of interest. A higher education class on leadership might use *The Intentional Leader* for basic understandings and skill development along with two or three other books and/or a number of articles that deal with issues in the field.

4. In-service training programs. As in the first example, using chapter 2 and then focusing on specific skill development areas could provide experi-

ences for trainees in business, government, and other areas where in-service training is encouraged.

5. Distance learning. While I haven't set the book up for use on the web, it could be used in situations where students are expected to read, complete assignments, and interact through electronic means. This idea is something I want to field test beyond the three students that helped me by reading and completing assignments in the manuscript. Perhaps you will beat me to it.

Selected Readings suggests books for use as supplements to *The Intentional Leader* or as main readings. Colleagues in various fields have helped me compile this list. No doubt you have others to add. Please share your thoughts with me. The more we help each other, the better we can advance the study of leadership.

Selected Readings

General Leadership

Bennis, Warren. *Why Leaders Can't Lead*. San Francisco: Jossey-Bass, 1989.

Carnegie, Dale. *The Leader in You: How to Win Friends and Influence People and Succeed in a Changing World*. New York: Simon and Schuster, 1993.

Coplin, William D. *How You Can Help: An Easy Guide to Doing Good Deeds in Your Everyday Life*. New York: Routledge, 2000.

Covey, Steven R. *Principle-Centered Leadership*. New York: Summit Books, 1990.

Gardner, Howard. *Changing Minds: The Art and Science of Changing Our Own and Other People's Minds*. Cambridge, Mass.: Harvard Business School Press, 2004.

Gardner, John. *On Leadership*. New York: Free Press, 1990.

Goleman, Daniel, Richard Boyatzis, and Annie McKee. *Primal Leadership: Learning to Lead with Emotional Intelligence*. Cambridge, Mass.: Harvard Business School Press, 2004.

Komives, Susan R., Nancy Lucas, and Timothy R. McMahon. *Exploring Leadership for College Students Who Want to Make a Difference*. San Francisco: Jossey-Bass, 1998.

Lee, Robert J., and Sara N. King. *Discovering the Leader in You*. San Francisco: Center for Creative Leadership and Jossey Bass, 2001.

Business Leadership

Bolman, Lee G., and Terrence E. Deal. *Reframing Organizations: Artistry, Choice, and Leadership*. 3d ed. San Francisco: John Wiley, 2003.

Collins, Jim. *Good to Great: Why Some Companies Make the Leap and Others Don't*. New York: Harper, 2001.

Coplin, William D., and Michael K. O'Leary. *Power Persuasion: A Surefire Way to Get Ahead in Business*. Reading, Mass.: Addison-Wesley, 1985.

Drucker, Peter F. *The Essential Drucker*. Cambridge, Mass.: Harvard Business School Press, 2001.

DuBrin, Andrew J. *The Complete Idiot's Guide to Leadership*. 2d ed. Indianapolis, Ind.: Alpha Books, 2000.

——. *Leadership: Research Findings, Practices, and Skills*. 4th ed. New York: Houghton Mifflin, 2004.

Gerstener, Louis V. *Who Says Elephants Can't Dance? Inside IBM's Historic Turnaround*. Cambridge, Mass.: Harvard Business School Press, 2002.

Kouzes, James M., and Barry Z. Posner. *The Leadership Challenge*. 3d ed. San Francisco: Jossey-Bass, 2002.

Northouse, Peter G. *Leadership: Theory and Practice*. Thousand Oaks, Calif.: Sage, 2003.

Schein, Edgar H. *Organizational Culture and Leadership*. San Francisco: Jossey-Bass, 2004.

Tichy, Noel M., and Eli B. Cohen. *The Leadership Engine: How Winning Companies Build Leaders at Every Level*. New York: HarperCollins, 2002.

Government and Public Affairs

Alinsky, Saul D. *Rules for Radicals: A Practical Primer for Realistic Radicals*. New York: Vintage Books, 1989.

Ambrose, Stephen E. *Eisenhower: The President*. New York: Simon and Schuster, New York, 1984

Burns, James MacGregor. *Leadership*. New York: Harper and Row, 1978.

Cannadine, David, ed. *Blood, Toil, Tears, and Sweat: The Speeches of Winston Churchill*. Boston: Houghton Mifflin, 1989.

Crislip, David D., and Carol E. Larson. *Collaborative Leadership: How Citizens and Civic Leaders Can Make a Difference*. San Francisco: Jossey-Bass, 1994.

Giuliani, Rudolph. *Leadership*. New York: Mirimax Books, 2002.

Goldsmith, Barbara. *Other Powers: The Age of Suffrage, Spiritualism, and the Scandalous Victoria Woodhull*. New York: Knopf, 1998.

Heifitz, Ronald A. *Leadership Without Easy Answers*. Cambridge, Mass: Harvard Univ. Press, 1984.

Hesselbein, Frances, and Eric K. Shinseki. *Be—Know—Do: Leadership in the Army*. San Francisco: Jossey-Bass, 2004.

Keegan, John. *The Mask of Leadership*. New York: Penquin Books, 1987.

King, Martin Luther, Jr. *Letters from the Birmingham Jail*. San Francisco: Harper, 1994.

Kopp, Wendy. *One Day All Children . . . : The Unlikely Triumph of Teach for America and What I Learned along the Way*. New York: Perseus Books, 2001.

Machiavelli, Niccolo. *The Prince*. Edited by Quentin Skinner and Russell Price. Cambridge: Cambridge Univ. Press, 1992.

Mandela, Nelson. *Long Walk to Freedom: The Autobiography of Nelson Mandela*. Boston: Back Bay Books, 1995.

Marshall, George C. *Memoirs of My Service in the War*. Boston: Houghton Mifflin, 1976.

McCullough, David. *Great Bridge: The Epic Story of the Building of the Brooklyn Bridge*. New York: Simon and Schuster, 1983.

———. *John Adams*. New York: Simon and Schuster, 2001.

———. *Truman*. New York: Simon and Schuster, 1993.

Pressfield, Steven. *Gates of Fire: An Epic Novel of the Battle of Thermopylae*. New York: Bantam Books, 1999.

Shaara, Michael. *The Killer Angels*. New York: Random House, 1975.

Higher Education

Birnbaum, Robert. *How Academic Leadership Works: Understanding Success and Failure in the College Presidency*. San Fransisco: Jossey-Bass, 1992.

Bornstein, Rita. *Legitimacy in the Academic Presidency: From Entrance to Exit*. Westport, Conn.: Praeger, 2003.

Bowen, William, and Harold Shapiro, eds. *Universities: Their Leadership.* Princeton, N.J.: Princeton Univ. Press, 1995.

Budig, Gene A. *A Game of Uncommon Skill: Leading the Modern College and University.* Phoenix, Ariz.: Oryx Press, 2002.

Crowley, Joseph N. *No Equal in the World: An Interpretation of the Academic Presidency.* Reno: Univ. of Nevada Press, 1994.

Diamond, Robert, ed. *Field Guide to Leadership.* San Francisco: John Wiley, 2002.

Fisher, James L. *The Power of the Presidency.* New York: American Council on Education/Macmillan, 1984.

Fisher, James L., and James V. Koch. *The Entrepreneurial College President.* Westport, Conn.: ACE/Praeger, 2004.

———. *Presidential Leadership: Making a Difference.* Phoenix, Ariz.: Oryx Press, 1996.

Sample, Steven B. *The Contrarian's Guide to Leadership.* San Francisco, Jossey-Bass, 2002.

Shaw, Kenneth A. *The Successful President: Buzz Words on Leadership.* Phoenix, Ariz.: Oryx Press, 1999.

Education

Argyris, Chris. *Strategy, Change and Defensive Routines.* Boston: Pitman, 1985.

Bolman, Lee G., and Terrence E. Deal. *Reframing Organizations.* San Francisco: Jossey-Bass, 1991.

Deal, Terrence E., and Kent D. Peterson. *Shaping School Culture: The Heart of Leadership.* San Francisco: Jossey-Bass, 1998.

Fullan, Michael G., ed. *Jossey Bass Reader on Educational Leadership.* San Francisco: Jossey-Bass, 2000.

———. *Leading in a Culture of Change.* San Francisco: Jossey-Bass, 2001.

Gordon, David. *The Myths of School Self-Renewal.* New York: Teachers College Press, 1984.

Jackall, Robert. *Moral Mazes: The World of Corporate Managers.* New York: Oxford Univ. Press, 1988.

Meier, Deborah. *The Power of Their Ideas: Lessons for America from a Small School in Harlem.* Ashland, Ohio: Beacon Press, 2002.

Moss Kanter, Rosabeth, et al. *The Challenge of Organizational Change.* New York: Free Press, 1992.

Senge, Peter M. *Schools That Learn: A Fifth Discipline Fieldbook for Educators, Parents, and Everyone Who Cares about Education.* New York: Doubleday, 2000.

Sizer, Theodore R. *Horace's Compromise.* Boston: Houghton Mifflin, 1997.

———. *Horace's School: Redesigning the American High School.* Boston: Houghton Mifflin, 1996.

Communication

Arledge, Roone. *Roone: A Memoir.* New York: HarperCollins, 2003.

Baldoni, John. *Great Communications Secrets of Great Leaders.* Columbus, Ohio: McGraw-Hill, 2003.

Bibb, Porter. *It Ain't as Easy as It Looks: Ted Turner's Amazing Story.* New York: Crown, 1993.

Chenoweth, Neil. *Rubert Murdoch: The Untold Story of the World's Greatest Media Wizard.* New York: Crown, 2002.

Clampitt, Phillip G. *Communicating for Managerial Effectiveness.* 3d ed. Thousand Oaks, Calif.: Sage, 2004.

Clarke, Boyd, and Ron Crossland. *The Leader's Voice: How Your Communication Can Inspire Action and Get Results.* New York: Select Books, 2002.

Croteau, David, and William Hoynes. *Media/Society: Industries, Images, and Audiences.* 3d ed. Thousand Oaks, Calif.: Sage, 2002.

Goodman, Michael B. *Corporate Communications for Executives.* Albany: State Univ. of New York, 1998.

Hackman, Michael Z., and Craig E. Johnson. *Leadership: A Communication Perspective.* 4th ed. Long Grove, Ill.: Waveland Press, 2003.

Mai, Robert, and Alan Akerson. *The Leader as Communicator: Strategies and Tactics to Build Loyalty, Focus, Effort, and Spark Creativity.* New York: AMACOM, 2003.

Pearce, Terry. *Leading Out Loud: Inspiring Change Through Authentic Communication.* San Francisco: Jossey-Bass, 2003.

Smith, Sally Bedell. *In All His Glory: The Life and Times of William S. Paley and the Birth of Modern Broadcasting.* New York: Random House, 2002.

Index

Page number in italic denotes either a figure or table.

217